OCR BUSINESS & COMMUNICATIONS SYSTEMS *for* GCSE

COLIN HARBER-STUART
NINA REES

Acknowledgements

The authors and publishers would like to thank the following for permission to reproduce copyright material.

Jupiterimages/Polka Dot/Alamy for picture on page 30; picture on page 47 © Trevor Norman / iStockphoto.com; Noel Vasquez/Getty Images for the picture on page 53; ColorBlind Images/Iconica/Getty Images for the picture on page 54 (top); Kim Steele/Alamy for the picture on page 54 (bottom); picture on page 61 ©iStockphoto.com/Dino Ablakovic; Hugh Threlfall/Alamy for the picture on page 64; Goodness Direct for the screen shot on page 79; Monica Rodriguez/ The Image Bank/Getty Images for the picture on page 88; Matt Cardy/Getty Images for the picture on page 89; Photodisc/Getty Images for the picture on page 95. Microsoft product screen shots reprinted with permission from Microsoft Corporation. Adobe product screen shots reprinted with permission from Adobe Systems Incorporated.

Every effort has been made to trace and acknowledge ownership of copyright. The publishers will be gald to make suitable arrangements with any copyright holders whom it has not been possible to contact.

Orders: please contact Bookpoint Ltd, 130 Milton Park, Abingdon, Oxon OX14 4SB.
Telephone: (44) 01235 827720.
Fax: (44) 01235 400454.
Lines are open from 9.00 – 5.00, Monday to Saturday, with a 24 hour message answering service. You can also order through our website www.hoddereducation.co.uk

> If you have any comments to make about this, or any of our other titles, please send them to educationenquiries@hodder.co.uk

British Library Cataloguing in Publication Data
A catalogue record for this title is available from the British Library

ISBN: 978 0 340 98443 7

First Edition Published 2009
Impression number   10 9 8 7 6 5 4 3 2 1
Year   2013 2012 2011 2010 2009

Copyright © 2009 Colin Harber-Stuart and Nina Rees

All rights reserved. No part of this publication may be reproduced or transmitted in any form or by any means, electronic or mechanical, including photocopy, recording, or any information storage and retrieval system, without permission in writing from the publisher or under licence from the Copyright Licensing Agency Limited. Further details of such licences (for reprographic reproduction) may be obtained from the Copyright Licensing Agency Limited, Saffron House, 6–10 Kirby Street, London EC1N 8TS.

Hachette UK's policy is to use papers that are natural, renewable and recyclable products and made from wood grown in sustainable forests. The logging and manufacturing processes are expected to conform to the environmental regulations of the country of origin.

Cover photo © Mustafa Deliormanli/iStockphoto.com
Typeset by Dorchester Typesetting Group Ltd
Printed and bound in Italy for Hodder Education, an Hachette UK Company, 338 Euston Road, London NW1 3BH

Contents

UNIT 1: BUSINESSES AND THEIR COMMUNICATION SYSTEMS   1

Section 1A: The business context   2

1.1	Why would anyone start a new business?	2
1.2	The main types of business organisation	4
1.3	How are businesses organised?	7
1.4	Business – success and failure?	10
1.5	Doing business in an uncertain world	12
1.6	Ensuring good relationships with customers (1): the importance of customers and monitoring customer satisfaction	14
1.7	Ensuring good relationships with customers (2): measuring customer satisfaction	17
1.8	Ensuring good relationships with customers (3): customer service	19
1.9	Competition (1): measuring business competitiveness	21
1.10	Competition (2): how to become more competitive	24
1.11	The legal framework (1): employment law	26
1.12	The legal framework (2): health and safety at work	29
1.13	The legal framework (3): consumer protection	32
1.14	The legal framework (4): data protection and access to information	34
1.15	The legal framework (5): copyright and computer misuse	37
1.16	The legal framework (6): environmental protection	40
1.17	Ethics and social responsibility	42

Section 1B: Introduction to communication systems   44

1.18	Procedures for checking internal and external business communications	44
1.19	Manual and computer-based systems (1): manual	47
1.20	Manual and computer-based systems (2): computer-based systems	50
1.21	Input devices (1)	52
1.22	Input devices (2)	54
1.23	Output devices (1)	57

1.24	Output devices (2)	59
1.25	Computing devices (1)	61
1.26	Computing devices (2)	63
1.27	Storage devices (1)	66
1.28	Storage devices (2)	69
1.29	Back-up systems	71
1.30	Data security (1)	74
1.31	Data security (2)	76
1.32	Data security (3)	78
1.33	Systems to support e-commerce (1)	80
1.34	Systems to support e-commerce (2)	82
1.35	Preparing for the examination	84

UNIT 2: DEVELOPING BUSINESS COMMUNICATION SYSTEMS 87

2.1	Business communication systems	88
2.2	Business communication methods	90
2.3	Internal business communication (1)	93
2.4	Internal business communication (2)	95
2.5	External business communication (1)	97
2.6	External business communication (2)	99
2.7	Communication devices (1)	101
2.8	Communication devices (2)	103
2.9	Stakeholders	105
2.10	The role of business communication systems in the success or failure of organisations	108
2.11	Capabilities and limitations of ICT-based systems	110
2.12	Changing business communication systems (1)	112
2.13	Changing business communication systems (2)	115
2.14	The controlled assessment	117

UNIT 3: ICT SKILLS FOR BUSINESS COMMUNICATION SYSTEMS — 119

3.1	Producing straightforward business documents using a word processor (business letters, memoranda, documents for a formal business meeting, documents for a training/conference event)	120
3.2	Creating simple images and logos using graphics software	129
3.3	Creating complex business documents using Desk Top Publishing Software	132
3.4	Creating business presentations using presentation software	138
3.5	Producing web pages using web-creation software	143
3.6	Analysing numerical information using a spreadsheet	146
3.7	Storing and managing customer and product records using a database	154
3.8	Organising diaries and meetings using diary management software	163
3.9	Managing projects using project management software	165
3.10	Sharing information on the web using *blogs* and *wikis*	167
3.11	Preparing for the examination	170

INDEX — 173

UNIT 1

BUSINESSES AND THEIR COMMUNICATION SYSTEMS

Section 1A: The business context

Topic 1.1

▸ Why would anyone start a new business?

Aims

By the end of this topic you should be able to:
- describe the main reasons for starting a business.

Why start a business?

Every year in the UK approximately 400,000 new businesses are started – that's over a thousand a day! However, around a fifth of these new businesses do not survive beyond their first year. So, why would anyone want to start a business?

There are several reasons why people choose to start a new business:

1 The desire to be your own boss
Many people start a business because they want to be independent. Sometimes this is because they do not like working for an employer and having managers telling them what to do. People often think that owning your own business will help them to escape the daily grind of working for someone else.

2 Personal fulfilment
Running your own business can be scary. The owner is responsible for the success or failure of the business so needs to know about everything that could affect how it performs. Some people see this as an opportunity to develop themselves by learning new ideas and skills.

3 To provide a product or service
Many people say that they started their business because they could not find the product or service it offers and so they decided to make it themselves! Other people decide to turn their hobby into a business.

4 Making money
Some people see running a business as their route to making a fortune. Del Boy in the BBC television series *Only Fools and Horses* frequently told his brother Rodney that 'next year we'll be millionaires'.

5 Lack of alternatives
All the above reasons are *positive motivators* for starting a business. Some people start a business for the *negative* reason that they find it difficult to get a job. This might be because they live in an area where jobs are scarce or it might be because of other reasons such as their age.

Activity

What would motivate you to run your own business? Put the five reasons listed above into an order of preference. Are there any other reasons you might have for starting a business?

Definition

An entrepreneur is someone who owns and operates their own business.

What does it take to be a successful entrepreneur?

Owning a business is a risky exercise. If the business is successful, the owner is likely to make a lot of money; but if the business is a failure they risk losing the money they have invested.

Entrepreneurs are likely to have the following characteristics:

- *Perseverance*
  When running a business, things sometimes do not work out as planned. It is important that the entrepreneur is prepared to keep trying to make the business a success. Equally, if the business is a failure it is important to know when to stop!

- *The desire and willingness to take the initiative*
  Remember, being an entrepreneur means being your own boss. Nobody is going to tell them how to run their business.

- *Competitiveness and a strong need to achieve*
  The entrepreneur is likely to be in competition with other businesses, so it is important that they have the desire to be better than the other firms in the market.

- *Self-confidence*
  Entrepreneurs need to believe in their own ability to succeed.

- *Toughness*
  Running your own business is hard work. Whilst you don't need to be physically fit to run every business, entrepreneurs do need to be prepared for the long hours that are involved.

Research task

There are many websites that offer online quizzes to test whether you have what it takes to be an entrepreneur. Put the keywords 'entrepreneur' (make sure you spell it correctly) and 'quiz' into an internet search engine and have a go at one of the quizzes you find. Do you have what it takes? If not, what do you need to develop?

Tasks

1. Are the following sentences true or false? You can find the answers in the text above. If they are false, write out the correct version.
   a. Every year in the UK approximately 400,000 new businesses are started.
   b. Every year in the UK, approximately four-fifths of these businesses fail by the end of their first year.
   c. An entrepreneur is someone who operates a business that is owned by someone else.

2. Jane Richards set up her sweet shop business in 2007 when she inherited some money. Since leaving school Jane has worked part-time in a local newsagents and has also spent time being unemployed. Jane did not enjoy working in the shop very much as she didn't like the way the shop was run. Whilst working in the newsagents Jane was asked several times by customers why there was no specialist sweet shop in the town. What reasons do you think Jane had for starting her own business?

3. Create your own quiz to help teenagers decide if they have what it takes to be a successful entrepreneur.

Topic 1.2

The main types of business organisation

Aims

By the end of this topic you should be able to:
- describe how a business is started
- describe the main features of business organisations and their benefits and drawbacks.

Most businesses exist to make a profit. This is achieved when the income the business receives from selling its products is greater than the costs it pays out to produce them and run the business. The owners of the business decide what to do with the profit, either to keep it in the business or take it out as their own personal reward. These businesses operate in the *private sector*.

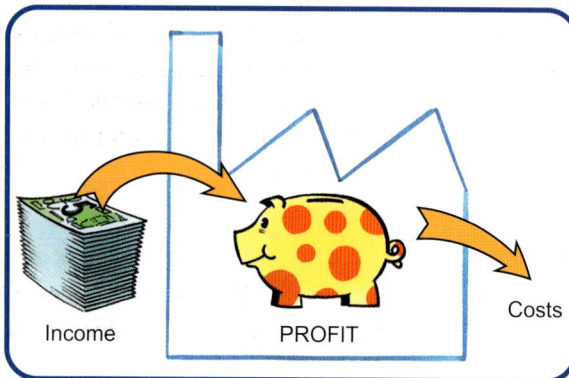

Owners of a business must decide what to do with profits

Some businesses are *not-for-profit* organisations. These include schools and hospitals which are owned by the government and therefore operate in the *public sector*. Other not-for-profit organisations include charities. As the name suggests, not-for-profit organisations do not aim to make a profit; however they are normally still required to cover their costs.

In the rest of this topic we will look at the main types of private sector profit-seeking business organisations.

Sole traders

These are the easiest type of businesses to set up. Anyone can become a sole trader by simply deciding to start operating as a business. Most small businesses start as a sole trader. Examples of sole traders include painters and decorators, plumbers and most people who run their own business from home.

Benefits
- Easy to set up: no forms to complete.
- Suitable for small businesses.
- The owner gets to keep all the profit.

Drawbacks
- Has *unlimited liability* which means if the business owes money the owner of the business is personally responsible for the full amount.
- Harder to raise money – banks are often reluctant to lend money to sole traders because they are considered to be too risky.

Partnerships

A partnership is a bit like a sole trader, except that it involves two or more people joined together to own a business. The rules and responsibilities of each partner, together with details of what share of the profits each partner receives, are usually contained in a *deed of partnership*. Doctors, accountants and architects often work together in partnerships.

Benefits
- More people to share work with.
- More money can be put into the business – new partners often join by 'buying' their share of the business.

Drawbacks
- Most partnerships have unlimited liability, though it is possible to have limited liability (see *Private Limited Companies* below).
- Making important decisions is difficult – it is hard to get every partner to agree on everything.

Private Limited Companies

A Private Limited Company has the abbreviation Limited (usually shortened to Ltd) after its name, e.g. Yorkshire Water Ltd.

Private Limited Companies are owned by *shareholders*. A single share represents one part of the ownership of a business. The more shares you own, the more control you have over how the business is run. The word private means that the shares are not openly traded; if you want to buy a share in a Private Limited Company you have to persuade individual shareholders to sell you their shares.

Ltds also have *limited liability*; the maximum amount any single shareholder can lose if the business fails is the amount they invested in the business.

Benefits
- Limited liability.
- Harder for the owners to lose control of the business, because they can control who does and does not own shares.
- Easier to raise money – banks are happier lending to Ltds than to sole traders.

Drawbacks
- Harder to set up than as a sole trader. The business must be registered with a government organisation called *Companies House.*
- More paperwork than a sole trader. The business must publish details of its financial performance every year.

Public Limited Companies

Public Limited Companies have the abbreviation PLC at the end of their names e.g. Tesco PLC. The main difference between a private and a public limited company is that anyone can buy shares in a PLC because they have to be traded on the London Stock Exchange. If someone decides to sell their shares then they will not know who they are selling them to. In this way it is relatively easy (if expensive!) for someone to take control of a PLC by buying enough shares.

Benefits
- Easier to raise money than other types of business, especially if done by selling new shares.
- ▉limited liability.

Drawbacks
- Individual shareholders often have little say in how the business is run, because there are so many of them.
- Harder for the existing owners to keep control of the business: they cannot control who owns the shares.

Franchises

Business such as McDonalds and Pizza Hut do not actually own the restaurants which sell their food. Instead, they sell their name, brand image and products to other organisations which then operate the restaurant as an independent business. In this example McDonalds is the franchisor and the business running a restaurant is called the franchisee. Franchising has benefits and drawbacks to both businesses.

Benefits and drawbacks to the franchisor

The business carries less risk as it doesn't actually own the outlets where its products are sold. It also has less control over some issues such as recruitment and quality control as these are managed by the franchisee.

Benefits and drawbacks to the franchisee

The business carries less risk as they are buying the right to sell the products of a well-known existing firm. It doesn't need to work at building up a brand-image because this has already been created. On the other hand the business will suffer from any problems caused by the franchisor; for example if the franchisor loses the public's confidence in its products then the franchisee's business may suffer a drop in sales through no fault of its own.

Tasks

1. Why do you think that most businesses that are started in the UK are sole traders?

2. Would you prefer to run a business that has limited or unlimited liability? Give a reason for your answer.

3. State one difference between a sole trader and a private limited company.

4. State one difference and one similarity between a private limited company and a public limited company.

5. Neil Armitage runs a business selling computers. Due to poor trading the business has been forced to close and owes its suppliers £56,000. Neil has personally invested £15,000 of his own money into the business. How much money would Neil lose if the business were a) A sole trader b) A private limited company?

6. Tariq Anwar made and sold his first computer game in 2005. His business now sells over 50,000 games a year and he employs 11 full-time staff. Tariq still operates his business as a sole trader. Write a report for Tariq explaining why it is not a good idea to continue as a sole trader. Explain what his options are for changing the business's ownership type and make a recommendation for which type he should adopt.

Topic 1.3

How are businesses organised?

Aims

By the end of this topic you should be able to:
- describe the main features of business organisations
- describe the main functional areas in a typical business
- explain the differences between a hierarchical and a flat organisation structure.

Functional areas

Whether they are large or small, all businesses need to carry out the same tasks in order to operate successfully. In large businesses such as Tesco PLC or Cadbury Schweppes PLC these activities are carried out by specialist staff working in *departments*. In smaller businesses such as a *sole trader* they can all be done by the same person – the owner. These tasks or departments can be divided up into a number of functional areas:

- *Purchasing*: buying the raw materials and products needed to operate the business and to produce the things it sells.

- *Production*: producing the business's *goods* or *services*.

- *Marketing*: making sure the business produces things that customers are prepared to buy.

- *Sales*: selling products to customers.

- *Customer service*: providing customers with after-sales service and dealing with their complaints.

- *Human resources*: recruiting people to work for the business then ensuring that the work they do is to the required standard.

- *Finance*: keeping records of all the money that flows into and out of the business; summarising how much profit or loss has been made and estimating how much the business is worth.

Definition

Goods are physical things produced by businesses that customers can buy and then own. Examples include cars, computers and cans of drink. Services are activities such as banking or babysitting that the business provides and customers pay to use.

Hierarchical structures

How is your school organised? Are some teachers in more senior positions than others? How many people are in charge of the whole school? Chances are, your school has a hierarchical organisation structure with the headteacher at the top, followed by at least one senior teacher, all the way down to classroom teachers.

In hierarchical organisations the people at the top have power over the people below them. In *limited companies* the most powerful people are the *directors*, followed by *managers*, then *supervisors* and finally *operatives*. Directors take decisions that affect the overall direction of the business (e.g. whether to bring out a new product or close down part of the business). The most senior director is called the Managing Director. *Managers* take the main decisions that affect the running of their functional area or department (e.g. who should be the members of a team developing a new product idea). *Supervisors* are responsible for the performance of a group of operatives (e.g. a sales supervisor in a shop is responsible for making sure that their team of sales staff do their jobs properly). Finally, *operatives* have no responsibility over other workers and simply have to perform the tasks that are given to them.

Hierarchical structures have a number of benefits:

- All staff know who they are responsible to.
- Communications can pass up and down a line, e.g. the sales director could hold a meeting with their sales managers who in turn report the messages to their sales supervisors who then tell the operatives.
- Directors, managers and supervisors are only directly responsible for a small number of people (the number of people someone is responsible for is known as the *span of control*).
- Hierarchical structures make it easier to control large organisations.

They also have drawbacks:

- A hierarchy can have many layers (the business in the diagram below has four layers). Large businesses can have several different layers of managers. The more layers, the longer the *chain of command*.
- Long chains of command can make communication difficult between the top and bottom of the hierarchy. For example, directors can find it hard to find out what operatives think about the business and messages passing along the chain can become distorted, rather like a game of chinese whispers.

Flat structures

To solve the problems of hierarchies, some organisations have flat structures. To do this they *de-layer* the business by removing layers of management and ask workers to operate in larger teams with fewer supervisors. Flat structures have the benefit of a smaller *chain of command* but the drawback is that the managers who remain have a wider *span of control*.

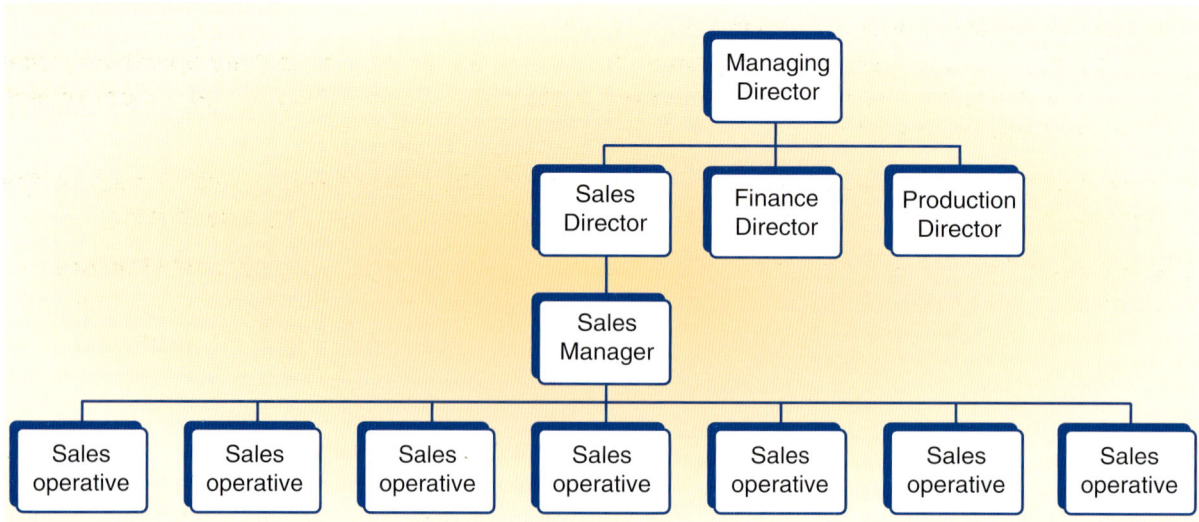

An organisation chart for a hierarchical organisation

How are businesses organised?

Tasks

1 Rewrite the following table so that the correct functional area is assigned to each task.

Functional area	Task
Finance	Recruiting people to fill a job vacancy
Production	Buying raw materials
Purchasing	Recording how much money the business earned yesterday
Sales	Turning raw materials into a finished product
Marketing	Explaining to a potential customer the benefits of buying the firm's products
Human resources	Giving advice to a customer who thinks the product they have just bought is faulty
Customer service	Writing a questionnaire to find out how much people would be prepared to pay for a new product

2 Explain two differences between how a small business is organised compared with a larger firm.

3 Bob Jones is a Production Director in a large bakery. Bob is responsible for four bakery managers and two other managers. There are no supervisors. Bob is responsible to the Managing Director, Karen Dickinson.
   a How wide is Bob's span of control?
   b How many layers does the organisation have?
   c If a number of supervisors are appointed to oversee the work of the bakery operatives, what will this do to the organisation's chain of command? Will the bakery become more or less hierarchical as a result?

4 How could the organisation structure of your school be made flatter? What would be the benefits and drawbacks of this change? Overall, do you think it would be a good idea?

5 Investigate a local business. How is it organised? Try to sketch its organisational structure.

Topic 1.4

Business – success and failure?

Aims

By the end of this topic you should be able to:
- describe the main features of business organisations
- evaluate why business organisations might succeed or fail in a given situation.

All businesses aim to be successful, but they don't always succeed. Businesses measure their success against their *objectives*, but for all businesses the most important objectives are to make a profit and survive.

Profit: the most important objective

The most important aim for any business (apart from not-for-profit organisations) is to make a profit. Profit is the owner's reward for investing their time, energy and money into the business. Part of the profit is also kept within the business and used to *invest* in its future, for example by funding the *expansion* of a manufacturing business by building a larger factory. Businesses that are not profitable (are loss-making) can only survive if they can persuade someone to invest or lend them money. Without this extra money the business will not be able to pay all its bills and so it may be declared *bankrupt* and be forced to close.

Other objectives

Survival

Government figures suggest that, in the UK, approximately one-third of new businesses cease trading within the first three years, so simply surviving is an important aim for new firms.

Market share

Market share is the proportion of money spent by customers in a particular market that is earned by a specific business. It can be worked out using the following formula:

Market share = the value of the business's sales/ total sales in that market X 100.

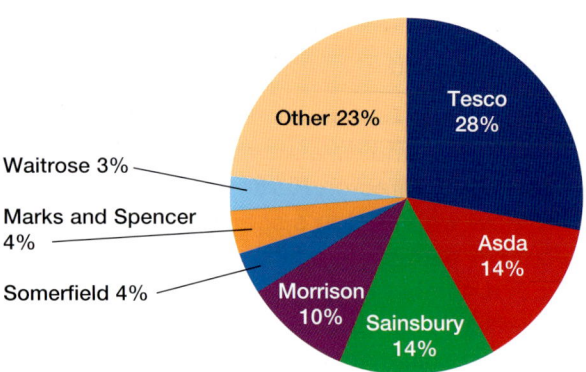

UK supermarkets: market share for 2007
Source: Competition Commission Groceries Market Investigation Final Report

A large market share is evidence that the business is successful because it sells products that many customers in the market choose to buy. It means the firm is performing better than its *competitors*.

Customer satisfaction

Some businesses believe that it is important for their survival that customers are happy with the goods and services they provide. They believe that happy customers are more likely to recommend them to other people and keep using the business in future. You will study how firms measure and try to improve their customer service in a later topic.

Reasons for business success

Businesses can succeed for a number of reasons including:

- having products that customers want to buy. This often comes from having a good market research department who really understand their customers and what they want from the product
- being able to charge the maximum price that customers are happy to pay. The easiest way to sell your product is to give it away for nothing – but this won't make you any profit
- staying one step ahead of the competition. Successful firms are aware of what their rivals are doing and can stay one step ahead of them, e.g. by bringing out new products
- having a good relationship with suppliers. Suppliers are important, especially for manufacturers as they supply them with raw materials
- a good location. This is especially important for retailers who need to have a steady flow of potential customers walking past their shop
- employing high-quality staff and making them feel valued.

Reasons for business failure

Failing to do the above things can cause problems for any business, but the biggest reason that businesses fail is poor *cash flow*. This happens when the business simply runs out of money to pay its suppliers, employees and pay back money it has borrowed. This happens either because customers stop buying its products or because of bad decisions such as buying too many raw materials.

Tasks

1. Complete the following sentence: a business that receives more money from selling its products than it pays out to operate the business is said to make a _____ .

2. Business X sells £10 million of products in a year. The total value of similar products sold by other firms was £90 million. What was business X's percentage share of the total market?

3. It has been suggested that Tesco PLC is the UK's most successful supermarket business. What reasons can you give to explain why Tesco is such a successful supermarket business?

4. Carry out research in newspapers or using on line news sources such as www.bbc.co.uk to find examples of businesses that have closed in the past six months. What reasons were given for their poor performance? Are there any factors which seem to be common to most of the businesses?

Topic 1.5

Doing business in an uncertain world

Aims

By the end of this topic you should be able to:
- evaluate why business organisations might succeed or fail in a given situation
- assess the impact of uncertainty on business organisations.

Dealing with uncertainty

None of us can be certain what the future holds. You might have chosen your GCSEs because of what you expect to be doing in five years' time, but can you really be certain what will happen during that time? Businesses face the same problem; a firm might decide to employ more production staff because it expects to sell more products over the coming year, but what happens if the expected sales fail to happen?

Examples of uncertainty

- Changes in the market: In 2008 the number of people buying new homes in the UK dropped dramatically and unexpectedly. As a result major house-builders such as Persimmon and Wimpey were forced to stop building new houses and make tens of thousands of workers redundant. Some smaller house-builders were unable to cope with the loss of income from not being able to sell houses they had built and ceased trading.

- Increased competition: In 2008, after years of heavy ticket demand, the owners of the Glastonbury music festival complained of poor ticket sales. This was blamed on rising competition from the many other music festivals that had developed to cater for people unable to get tickets for the sell-out Glastonbury concerts.

- External influences: These include other things that businesses cannot directly control. For example in August 2008 the airline British Airways announced that its profits had fallen by 80% in one year. It blamed the fall in profits on a large increase in the cost of aircraft fuel.

The main external influences can be summarised as follows:

1 Political: Decisions made by governments can affect businesses. For example, governments pass *laws* which must be followed by businesses. Later in this book you will study some of the main laws which businesses must follow.

2 Economic: The economy can be defined as the system that enables goods and services to be made and then bought and sold. Businesses are affected by the state of the economy. For example, in 2008 the rise in the cost of airline fuel was blamed on increased demand for oil from China and India; this increased the price of oil. Oil is an important raw material used in many industries (as well as being used to make petrol and diesel). As a result many businesses found their costs increased and so they had to increase the price they charged customers.

3 Social: Changes in society affect businesses. For example, the average age in the UK is getting older as people are living longer. As a result many businesses are responding by targeting their products at older customers. A good example is Virgin, owned by the entrepreneur Sir Richard Branson. The business started over 30 years ago selling music to young people and now sells a range of products which mainly target the 30-55 age range. A second way that social changes affect business is changes in people's lifestyles. For example, a growing number of people in the UK prefer to buy food which is grown in their local area. As a result, many farms now operate their own farm shops, selling their food directly to the public.

4 Technological: Changes in technology affect business. Businesses are both users as well as producers of technology. Around the world millions of people are directly employed in thousands of businesses that simply did not exist thirty years ago, because the technology they use or sell did not exist. Examples include mobile telephone suppliers and businesses that trade over the internet.

Much of the rest of this book describes how business communications are affected by new technologies.

Responding to uncertainty

Businesses need to be aware of the changes happening in the world around them. They need to decide what action to take in order to respond to the changes that affect them. These responses can include:

- reducing costs or increasing prices. For example, in response to the increase in oil prices in 2008, petrol stations were forced to increase their prices.

- bringing out new products or changing existing ones. For example, for many years car manufacturers have attempted to design vehicles that run on alternatives to petrol or diesel. This is because they are aware that the world will one day run out of oil.

Tasks

1 State whether the following are examples of political, economic, social or technological influences on business behaviour:
   a Since 2007, all workplaces in England and Wales are required to be 'smoke-free' by banning cigarette smoking on the premises.
   b Between 2004 and 2008 use of the internet increased by over 400%.
   c In 2008 many people became worried that they faced an increased risk of losing their job. As a result they spent less and saved more.
   d Over the past ten years the proportion of people choosing to get married has fallen. The numbers choosing to get married in a church has fallen, and more people are choosing to get married in stately homes, castles and hotels.

2 In 2008 a number of UK house-builders stopped building new homes; some ceased trading altogether. Identify and explain reasons why this might have happened.

3 Carry out research using newspapers or using online news sources to find examples of businesses that have reported problems in the past six months. What reasons were given for their poor performance? Group these reasons according to whether they are political, economic, social or technological.

4 Take any two of the businesses you have researched in Task 3 and recommend actions they could take to respond to their changed circumstances.

Topic 1.6

Ensuring good relationships with customers (1): the importance of customers and monitoring customer satisfaction

Aims

By the end of this topic you should be able to:
- describe why customers are important to the success of business organisations.

Most businesses's main aim is the need to make a profit. In this topic you will learn about the crucial importance of customers to business organisations.

Why do customers matter?

Think about the things you and your household buy every week and how much they all cost. In 2007 a typical family spent £100 each week in supermarkets – that's over £5,000 a year! From the household perspective that is money spent, but from the supermarket's viewpoint, it is income received.

Research task

How much money does your class spend in total in a typical week? Multiply this by 52. This is the total amount of money that businesses earn from your class every year.

Remember, in order to make a profit a business must earn more money than it pays out. The main source of business income is the money received from selling goods and services to customers. So, unless a business is successful in selling its products to customers it will struggle to earn enough money to cover its costs and make a profit. As a result, most businesses try to ensure that they develop good relationships with their customers and provide them with a high level of service.

Why measure customer satisfaction?

Businesses spend a lot of money finding out what customers think of them. This is because the markets where they operate are usually very competitive – there are often many different businesses attempting to persuade customers to buy from them instead of their competitors. Offering higher levels of customer service than your rivals can help to persuade customers to do business with you instead. Finding out what customers like and don't like about your businesses is often the first step towards taking action to improve levels of customer care.

Methods of measuring customer satisfaction

There are a number of different methods that a business can use to measure the level of customer satisfaction with the business.

- **Monitoring the number of customer complaints**
  Many businesses operate customer support telephone lines. By monitoring the number of calls to these lines they will obtain useful information about customer satisfaction. Of course, not every customer who has a problem will call a support line, but a sudden increase in the number of such calls should alert the business to the possibility of a problem.

- **Customer panels or interviews e.g. sales follow-up interviews**
  Many businesses arrange to contact customers a few weeks after they have bought a product to ask them about the level of customer service they received. This is especially common with sellers of expensive products, such as car dealerships. Other businesses will arrange for a group of customers to meet together and talk with them about what they think of the business and its customer service. These groups are sometimes called *panel interviews* or *focus groups*. Sometimes a business will meet the same focus group at regular intervals over a number of months or even years, in order to find out how the opinions of the group members change over time.

- **Questionnaires**
  This is a popular method of obtaining customer feedback. An example is the hotel industry, where feedback forms are often left in hotel rooms and guests are encouraged to complete them and return them to the hotel reception. Questions usually ask customers about: their experiences booking the room; checking in at the hotel; the quality of their room and the other facilities offered by the hotel.

Tasks

1. Explain why customers are important to the success of business organisations.
2. Explain, in your own words, why businesses should be aware of what their customers think of them.
3. Higgins Boats Limited manufactures and sells luxury yachts. Identify and explain two methods the business could use to find out what customers think of the quality of its after-sales service.
4. Write a questionnaire that could be used to find out what customers of a high street clothes shop think of its level of customer service.

Hotel Accommodation Survey

We hope you enjoyed your stay with us! To help us better serve you, please complete this survey and return it to the reception desk at your convenience. Thank you!

Statement	Strongly Agree	Agree	Neutral	Disagree	Strongly Disagree
My overall experience here was good, and I would recommend this hotel to my friends.					
Check in					
My booking details were accurate.					
The check-in process was timely and efficient.					
The check-in staff was courteous.					
Guest Room					
My room was clean and comfortable.					
My room was furnished appropriately.					
My bed and bedding were comfortable.					
Guest Staff					
The guest staff was prompt, reliable, and friendly.					
The guest staff was knowledgeable and fully answered my questions about the area.					
Security was available if needed.					
Housekeeping staff was friendly and reliable.					
Management was available to solve problems.					
Food and Dining					
The food and dining staff was courteous.					
The food quality was good.					
Room service was timely and efficient.					
Room service delivered the correct food order.					
Amenities					
Hotel amenities (pool, Jacuzzi, exercise room) were clean, attractive, and properly equipped.					
Check out					
The check-out process was timely and efficient.					
I received a complete and accurate bill.					
Additional Comments:					

Example of a hotel feedback form

Topic 1.7

Ensuring good relationships with customers (2): measuring customer satisfaction

Aims

By the end of this topic you should be able to:
- describe why customers are important to the success of business organisations
- evaluate the actions businesses can take in order to ensure good customer relationships.

Methods of measuring customer satisfaction

- **Website feedback**
  Some business websites include customer feedback forms, or have pop-up windows that invite every hundredth or thousandth visitor to complete a short online questionnaire. This can be a useful way of finding out what people think of the website or the business in general.

- **Secret shoppers**
  Asking customers what they think of the customer service received is very useful. However, it has the drawback of only telling the business what customers think; it doesn't tell the business what it is actually like to be one of their customers. Secret shoppers are employed by a business to visit the places where customers come into contact with the business and pretend to be a real customer. Sometimes they record their experiences using hidden cameras and microphones. Other times they simply record their experiences by writing them down. The business can then understand what it is like to be a customer, and seek to find ways to improve the experience. For example, a supermarket may have a policy that if there are more than five people queuing at a checkout then another checkout should be opened. Using secret shoppers, the supermarket can find out if this policy works in practice. Secret shoppers are also known as mystery shoppers.

- **Product testing**
  Testing the quality of the product with selected customers is a useful way of obtaining their feedback on its quality. For example, supermarket shoppers could be asked to do a 'taste test' by comparing similar types of soft drink without knowing which business has produced each one.

- **Benchmarking**
  It is not enough just to look at the performance of your own business. Customers are able to compare the levels of service offered by a number of different businesses, e.g. by shopping in different supermarket branches. Many businesses use techniques such as secret shoppers to find out about the levels of customer service offered by their competitors. Comparing your performance to the standards set by others is called *benchmarking*.

Customer service policies

Your school has expectations of how its students and teachers should work together. These expectations are probably written down and displayed in classrooms. In a similar way, many businesses have expectations of how its staff should act in order to provide a high level of service to its customers. These expectations are called *policies*. A policy is a statement of what the organisation expects its employees to do in certain circumstances. For example, it might have a telephone policy which sets out how it expects staff to act when using a telephone to speak with customers.

Customer service standards

Some organisations set standards they expect their staff to follow when working with customers. The following is an example of the standards typically in place at a public library:

- All returned books will be put back on shelves within six hours.
- All staff will wear name badges.
- All letters and emails to the library will be acknowledged within one day and dealt with within three days.
- Two-thirds of all incoming telephone calls will be answered within five rings.

Tasks

1. A music store sells 80% of its products via its website. Identify and describe three methods the business could use to find out what customers think of its level of service.

2. A food manufacturer is planning to produce a new low-fat version of an existing breakfast cereal. Identify and explain two methods the business could use to find out what customers think of the new product.

3. As part of a group, devise a strategy for finding out the quality of customer service offered by a business of your choice. Carry out the research and produce a short report of your findings. Present your findings to the rest of the class.

4. A new business is planning to allow potential customers to contact them by telephone with questions they might have about the business and its products. Produce a policy for how the business can ensure it provides customers with a good level of before-sales service. Include some service standards for dealing with incoming telephone calls.

Topic 1.8

Ensuring good relationships with customers (3): customer service

Aims

By the end of this topic you should be able to:
- **evaluate the actions businesses can take in order to ensure good customer relationships.**

Customer service

Customer service can be defined as the activities a business carries out before, during and after a customer buys a product from them.

Before the sale, the business can provide information and guidance to customers. For example a computer manufacturer can provide information about the main features of a computer as well as information on its selling price and how long it will take to deliver. This information could be provided in leaflets and brochures, in a shop, on a website, or by telephone.

During the sale the customer is likely to be speaking either with a sales person face-to-face or by telephone, or ordering a product online.

After the sale, the customer might have some queries (for example how the product works) or problems (such as the product not working correctly). Businesses provide after-sales services in a number of ways including: product guides that contain instructions and advice on how to solve simple problems; telephone help lines; and websites that provide additional information and support such as downloadable updates for computer software.

The impact of poor customer service

There are many ways in which customers can receive poor customer service. Some examples are listed below:

- Time spent waiting for help and advice. Some businesses employ people in *call centres* to speak to customers over the telephone. Some customers complain that the time they spend waiting to be connected to a call centre employee is too long. This might be because the business has an unexpectedly large number of people phoning them at the same time; or it might be a deliberate decision to employ too few staff.

- Sales staff who do not know enough about the products they sell. Some businesses may not provide enough training for their sales staff about the features of the products they sell. This may be difficult to achieve in businesses such as electrical stores which sell a large range of highly technical products. However, the consequence can sometimes be that customers are unable to have their questions answered.

- Poor quality or misleading information in product manuals. Some products such as computers or DVD recorders may be difficult to set up and use for the first time. Product manuals that do not use clear and straightforward language are likely to leave the customer feeling frustrated.

- Products that take longer to deliver than expected. This is a particular problem when buying products over the internet. For example some websites will not tell you whether a product is in stock and how long it will take to deliver until *after* you have placed your order.

Businesses which offer poor customer service are likely to see a fall in sales and as a result, a fall in income and profits. Poor *before-sales service* means that potential customers are less likely to buy their products from them and shop elsewhere instead. Research in the UK, for example, has shown that customers are reluctant to buy products from businesses which do not have websites providing advice and information about their products. Poor *after-sales service* means that customers are less likely to buy from the business again. Most successful businesses enjoy a large amount of *repeat business* from existing customers who are happy with the level of service they receive. Dissatisfied customers are also less likely to recommend the business to their friends. Research shows that *word-of-mouth recommendation* is one of the most effective ways for a business to increase its number of customers and hence sales income. This is especially true for new small businesses which provide a service to the public.

Tasks

1. What are the three main stages when customer service is carried out?

2. a Describe a recent example of good customer service you have received.
   b Describe a recent example of poor customer service you have received.
   c What impact have these different experiences had on your opinion of the businesses concerned and the likelihood you will buy from them again in the future?

3. Produce a short two-minute presentation for new employees at a clothes shop telling them of the importance to the business of good customer service before, during and after the sale.

4. Research a local business to find out how it monitors its relationships with customers. Make recommendations on how it could improve its levels of customer service.

Topic 1.9

Competition (1): measuring business competitiveness

Aims

By the end of this topic you should be able to:
- describe how a business can monitor the effectiveness of its own competitive position.

All businesses face competition from other firms. It is sometimes said that some businesses have what is called a *monopoly* by being the only supplier of a particular product. For example there is only one Channel Tunnel and if you want to travel from London to Paris by train then you have to use the one operated by a business called Eurostar. However, there are other ways of getting from London to Paris, including taking your car through the tunnel or using a ferry or flying. So in reality Eurostar may have a monopoly of travelling from London to Paris by train, but it is still competing with other businesses in the market for transporting people between the two cities.

Definition

A market is any situation where buyers and sellers are able to come together and trade a particular good or service. It does not have to be in a single place. Examples include the market for housing, the market for home computers and the market for transport between London and Paris.

Successful businesses are those which actively monitor how competitive they are compared with other firms in the same market.

Methods of monitoring competitiveness

- **Prices**

Many people will compare the prices of competing products before choosing which one to buy. If two products are identical then people will generally buy the cheapest. A quick way to compare the prices offered by different online suppliers is to use a price comparison website such as *kelkoo* or *pricerunner*. Sometimes the comparison is harder because different manufacturers' products are not identical. Examples include comparing two similar computers made by different manufacturers, or two cars made by different producers. In these cases consumers will choose the supplier whose product offers the best *value for money*. It is relatively easy for businesses to compare their own prices with those charged by their competitors – they can carry out *price surveys* by studying price lists, or by visiting their shops to record the prices charged. Sometimes it is harder and they might use secret shoppers.

- **Market share**

Market share was defined in Topic 1.4 as being the proportion of total spending in a particular market that was spent on a specified business or product. For example the market share of Microsoft's Windows computer operating system software has generally been over 90%. Market share data can be calculated once you know how much each firm in the market has sold. Businesses are generally quite secretive about such information because they know it is useful to their rivals. However, many businesses are still able to estimate their own market share with reasonable accuracy.

- **Market research**
Topics 1.6 and 1.7 described the methods used by businesses to find out what their customers think of the level of service they offer. Many of these methods can be used to carry out *market research* into how competitive a particular business is.

There are two main types of market research:

1. Field research (also called primary research): this is where the researcher obtains new information that nobody has collected before. Examples of field research methods include price surveys, questionnaires, interviews and focus group discussions.

2. Desk research (also called secondary research): this is where the researcher makes use of information that has already been collected and published by other people. Examples of desk research include: looking at the websites of competitors, reading market research reports published by organisations such as Mintel and studying newspapers and magazines.

Tasks

1 Explain the difference between desk research and field research.

2 Which of the following examples of research activities are examples of field research?
   a Devising and using a questionnaire.
   b Reading a report produced by a market research organisation.
   c Visiting a store owned by a competitor.
   d Watching a television programme about the travel industry.

3 Oxford Computers make and sell personal computers to customers throughout the United Kingdom. They have asked you to analyse some market research data and write a report explaining how competitive they currently are. The information you have been provided with is shown below:

Year	Market share (%)
2002	14%
2003	16%
2004	17%
2005	19%
2006	22%
2007	22%
2008	20%

Oxford Computers' share of the UK personal computer market, 2002–2008

Competition (1): measuring business competitiveness

Comments from focus group in 2004:
'When I had a problem the helpline staff were very friendly.'
'Your products are very well-built and haven't caused me any problems.'
'They're not the cheapest, but they're amongst the best.'

Comments from a focus group in 2009:
'I don't like the waiting times to speak to people at your new call centre.'
'You haven't brought out any new products for four months!'
'I had to return my last computer and it took four weeks to be repaired!'

Quotation from a recent market research report:
'The market for personal computers has grown rapidly over the past ten years and has recently become very competitive. Customers state that quality and reliability are becoming more important than price in determining their purchasing decisions.'

Questionnaire results, 2005 and 2009.

1. Customers very happy with our level of service: 78% (2005), 67% (2009).
2. People giving 'too expensive' as a reason for not purchasing our products: 55% (2005), 35% (2009).
3. People giving 'poor quality' as a reason for not recommending our products to friends: 35% (2005), 48% (2009).

Topic 1.10

Competition (2): how to become more competitive

Aims

By the end of this topic you should be able to:

- evaluate the actions a business can take in order to be more competitive than its rivals.

What should a business do if it learns that it is becoming less competitive? The answer will depend on the reasons why it is uncompetitive in the first place. However, it is likely that it will attempt some of the following:

- **Reduce the prices of existing products**
  Imagine that a car manufacturer discovers that its cars are £2,000 more expensive than those of its competitors. One response would be to lower its prices by just over £2,000. This would make its cars cheaper than those of its competitors so more customers would be expected to buy them. Lowering prices can be a good *short-term* way to make products more competitive. However, there are problems: one drawback is that competitors may respond by lowering their prices. This will leave the business worse off than before. Prices are still too high, but are now £2,000 lower, so the customers who are happy to buy their cars are giving them £2,000 less each time. This will lower the firm's income by £2,000 per car and so will lower the amount of profit the business makes. A second drawback is that the new price may be below the cost of producing each car. Cutting prices may make the business more competitive, but if it reduces profits it may make it harder for it to survive in the long run. A third drawback is that for some products, price is not a very important factor in influencing people's buying decisions. This is especially true for low-cost products. So lowering the price may not have a big impact on sales.

- **Improve the promotion of existing products**
  The most well-known method businesses use to promote their products is by *advertising* them, for example on television or in magazines. Common methods of promotion include advertising: adverts generally either provide *information* about a product or attempt to *persuade* people that it is worth buying. A common persuasion technique is to put the product in glamorous settings to make people think that using the product will help them to appear glamorous as well.

Research task

Watch a selection of TV adverts. Which ones are informative and which ones are persuasive?

- **Point-of-sale promotions**
  This includes using special display cases for the product which attract shoppers' eyes when they visit the shop. Point-of-sale promotion is used to encourage 'impulse-buying'.

- **Packaging**
  You may not think of the way a product is packaged as being part of the way it is promoted, but in reality, putting a product inside a well-designed, eye-catching wrapper or box will help persuade people to buy the product.

The main drawback with promotion activities is their cost. For example, placing an advert on one of the main TV channels in the UK can cost hundreds of thousands of pounds.

- **Develop new improved products**
  Most products eventually become out of date as tastes and fashions change. A business that fails to update its products will eventually find that customers stop buying them and move on to something new. A good example is cars, which often only have a *product life* of four or five years. After this time car-makers usually bring out a new improved version of the car, perhaps by altering the design or by adding new features. Then, typically, three or four years later the business stops making the car and replaces it with a new improved model. Each time a product is updated or replaced is an opportunity for the business to create a product which is better than those offered by its competitors.

A drawback with this approach is that it is very expensive to develop new products, so it isn't a solution that can be used very often. Another problem is that if the business makes a mistake with its new product it can be very expensive. For example a well-known soft-drinks manufacturer changed the recipe for its main product in the early 1980s, but unfortunately the public didn't like the taste and so sales of the new product fell.

- **Improve levels of customer service**
  Topic 1.8 looked at the range of activities a business might carry out to provide before, during and after-sales service to its customers. Improving customer service is one way of helping to make businesses more attractive to customers. A recent development is to improve the *speed of response* time it takes to deal with customer complaints.

Tasks

1 Explain why a business suffering from poor sales might wish to lower its prices.

2 Describe two reasons why lowering prices may not always be a good way to improve competitiveness.

3 Explain the difference between informative and persuasive advertising.

4 You are responsible for the introduction of a new brand of chocolate bar. Describe the point-of-sale activities you could use to promote the product.

5 Study the data given in Task 3, Topic 1.9. Recommend a range of actions the business should take to improve its competitiveness. Explain why you have chosen these actions and not others.

Topic 1.11

The legal framework (1): employment law

Aims

By the end of this topic you should be able to:
- describe the principles of employment law
- analyse the actions required of business organisations in order to comply with employment law
- evaluate the impact on business organisations of the need to comply with employment law.

All of us have to follow many different laws and regulations. Sometimes it seems there are so many rules it can be hard to remember all of them. The UK government has passed many different laws which affect the way that businesses can treat their workforce. In this topic we will look briefly at some of the main areas of employment law and consider the implications of these laws for businesses and their workers.

The main principle behind employment law is that it sets out exactly what an employer (a business which hires workers) can and cannot do to an employee (the person who is paid by the employer to work for them). Some of the main areas covered by employment law are as follows.

Recruitment

Recruitment is the process by which an employer first identifies they have a requirement for an additional worker, then recruits them by advertising the vacancy, inviting people to apply in writing, then studying the applications to select people for interview, before finally selecting the person who will be offered the job. UK employment law makes it illegal to discriminate against job applicants because of their age, gender, any disabilities, ethnic group, religion, sexual orientation or because they might be pregnant. In short, employers are required by law to appoint the applicant best suited to doing the job regardless of any other factors.

Pay and conditions

- All employees should be paid the same as their colleagues doing similar work of equal value. For example, a cleaner must receive the same pay as another cleaner doing the same job, if it can be proved that they both do work that is of equal value to the company.

- All employees are entitled to paid holidays (the legal minimum is four weeks though some employers offer more) and sick pay if they are too ill to work.

- Employers must provide a healthy and safe working environment (see Topic 1.12).

- Employers must not discriminate against any employee for the reasons given above.

- All employees are entitled to belong to a trade union (an organisation that represents employees and negotiates on their behalf with employers to decide things like pay levels).

Employees with families

- Parents are entitled to paid maternity (for mothers) and paternity (for fathers) leave to look after their newborn child.

The legal framework (1): employment law

- Mothers are entitled to paid leave from work in the weeks leading up to the birth of their baby and for a time afterwards.

Leaving employment

- Employers can make an employee *redundant* (meaning their job is no longer needed and so there is no reason to employ them) but only if they can prove the work is no longer required. The employer must use fair means to decide who to make redundant and who to keep and should explain these rules to the staff. Employers should provide sufficient notice to staff they are making redundant and compensate them with *redundancy pay*.

- Employers can dismiss a worker for breaking company rules, but only if the employer has a *discipline procedure* which they have followed. Most discipline procedures require the business to issue a verbal warning when the problem first occurs, then if the problem continues, a written warning will be issued. Finally, if the situation does not improve the employee can be dismissed from their post. *Instant dismissal* can be carried out if the offence is serious (e.g. physically assaulting a customer) and is therefore an example of *gross misconduct*.

- Employees can leave employment but they are also required to give a period of notice to the employer. This is usually a short period of weeks, e.g. four weeks' notice.

You can find out more about employment law and what it means for businesses and their employees at the official government website: www.direct.gov.uk/en/Employment/index.htm.

Implications for employers

The main impact of employment law on businesses is that it raises the cost of employing staff. For example, it costs money to pay staff whilst they are not working and on holiday, off sick or looking after a new baby. These increased costs may have to be recovered by, for example, cutting other costs such as employing fewer workers or raising prices to customers. On the other hand all employers have to implement employment law and so face similar costs; so it is unlikely that any single business will lose customers because it has to follow these laws.

Tasks

1. A male cleaner is paid more than a female cleaner. Is this legal?

2. A female shop assistant believes that she should be paid the same as a female delivery driver. What does the shop assistant have to do to receive the same pay?

3. All UK employees are entitled to a minimum of five weeks' holiday pay. True or false?

4. An employee arrives late for work every day. Describe the actions the business can take as part of a discipline procedure.

5. Which of the following would normally be grounds for instant dismissal?
   a Being more than five minutes late for work.
   b Being rude to a customer.
   c Accidentally deleting an important file.
   d Deliberately setting fire to the business.

6. A business wishes to make some of its workers redundant. Explain what 'redundancy' means and describe what the business must do in order to make workers redundant.

7. 'All businesses suffer because of the need to follow employment law.' Do you agree with this opinion? Give reasons for your answer.

Topic 1.12

The legal framework (2): health and safety at work

Aims

By the end of this topic you should be able to:
- describe the principles of health and safety legislation
- analyse the actions required of business organisations of the need to comply with health and safety legislation
- evaluate the impact on business organisations of the need to comply with health and safety legislation.

Accidents at work can cost time and money to put right as well as affecting people's lives. According to the Health and Safety Executive (HSE), the organisation responsible for health and safety in the UK, 36 million working days were lost in 2006/2007 due to injury, accident or poor health: that's an average of 1.5 days per worker. Everybody wants to feel safe at work, but who should be responsible for making sure the working environment is healthy and safe? Under UK law the responsibility lies with both the business (the employer) and the people who work for it (the employees).

The basic principle of health and safety legislation is to require businesses to take responsibility for the health and safety of their employees and other visitors to their workplaces. However, it also places some of the responsibility on employees to look after their own safety as well as the safety of others.

There are many different health and safety related laws and regulations that businesses must follow in the UK. However, two of the most important ones that apply to most businesses are:

Health and Safety at Work Act 1974

The main provisions of this law are that:

- employers are responsible for the health and safety of their employees and other users of their business premises (such as visitors and customers)
- employers should provide health and safety training and information to their employees, for example how to use a new piece of equipment safely
- employees are responsible for their own health and safety and that of other people that their work might affect; for example, a fork-lift truck driver should be aware of the movements of other workers in a warehouse.

The Act also set up the Health and Safety Executive (HSE) to be responsible for ensuring the law is followed by businesses.

There are a number of specific actions employers are required to carry out under this act. These include:

- carrying out a *risk assessment* of the workplace to identify any potential health and safety hazards, the extent of any potential injury resulting from the hazard and the chances of the event occurring. Action should then be taken to minimise the extent of any potential problem
- appointing health and safety officers to be responsible for seeing that the law is followed

- keeping an *accident book* to record health and safety incidents and, when required, to report them to the HSE.

Any business found guilty of breaking the Health and Safety at Work Act can be prosecuted and, if found guilty, can face an unlimited fine. In addition, any individual found guilty (for example a manager who forces an employee to disregard the Act) can face a prison sentence.

> You can find out more about health and safety legislation and what it means for businesses at the Health and Safety Executive website: www.hse.gov.uk.

The Health and Safety (Display Screen Equipment) Regulations 1992

These regulations apply to any workplace that requires workers to use computer display screens (this also includes equipment such as computerised cash registers that use a computer screen). Employers are required to:

- analyse the workstation where the display screen is used and identify any health and safety risks
- ensure that all equipment used by workers meets legal minimum health and safety standards; this includes providing adjustable computer chairs and suitable lighting
- plan the daily routine of their workers so that they are given breaks from using computer equipment; this can include giving them non-computer work to do
- provide regular eye-sight tests for employees who use computer display equipment
- provide information and training to employees in the healthy and safe use of computer display equipment, for example the correct way to sit when working at a computer workstation.

The correct posture for computer use

The impact of health and safety legislation

First of all, health and safety laws require businesses to take action to both monitor and respond to health and safety hazards. Some of these actions have been listed above. These actions will take money and time to carry out. The business may have to buy new equipment or require staff to receive training at a time when they would otherwise be doing their job. Health and safety officers may also need to be employed. All this will cost the business money and will help to increase its costs of doing business. Any action that raises business costs will also help to reduce profits. However, there are benefits of implementing health and safety legislation. A safe

The legal framework (2): health and safety at work

workplace might help employees to be more productive if, for example, they take fewer days off sick or suffer fewer workplace injuries. This will help to increase the amount the business produces and so can sell to customers. In addition, by meeting legal requirements the business will not be breaking the law, and so will not risk being taken to court and fined.

Tasks

1. Who is responsible for ensuring that a workplace is kept safe?
2. State four things that an employer must do to follow the Health and Safety at Work Act.
3. What is a risk assessment? Carry out a risk assessment of the place where you are working now.
4. An employee is required to use a computer for eight hours every day whilst at work. State three health problems that could result from this amount of computer use. Describe three actions that an employer should take to minimise the risk of the user developing health problems.
5. Describe the benefits and drawbacks to a business of following health and safety legislation. Do you think the overall impact on the business is good or bad? Give reasons for your answer.
6. Create an information leaflet designed to raise awareness of health and safety issues amongst office workers who regularly use computers.

Topic 1.13

The legal framework (3): consumer protection

Aims

By the end of this topic you should be able to:

- describe the principles of consumer protection legislation
- analyse the actions required of business organisations of the need to comply with consumer protection legislation
- evaluate the impact on business organisations of the need to comply with consumer protection legislation.

Over the years the government has created many different laws that all have the same aims: to set out the terms under which sellers can supply goods and services to customers, and to protect customers from unfair selling practices.

> Suppose you see an advert in a newspaper selling one kilogram of luxury chocolates for £3.99. You send the supplier a cheque along with your name and address. What could happen so you do not receive exactly what you ordered?

Some of the main laws protecting consumers are as follows:

- Sale of Goods Act 1979
- Supply of Goods and Services Act 1982
- Sale and Supply of Goods Act 1994
- The Consumer Protection (Distance Selling) Regulations 2000
- Sale and Supply of Goods to Consumers Regulations 2002.

Some of the main implications of these laws and regulations for businesses who supply goods or services are as follows:

- Products must be of *merchandisable quality*: in other words they must be *fit for purpose*. For example, a waterproof coat should keep out the rain and a watch must tell the time with reasonable accuracy. A box of luxury chocolates should be of a higher quality than 'ordinary' chocolates. A supplier of services should carry them out to a reasonable standard; for example a painter should paint just the walls of a house and not drip paint over carpets and furniture.

- Product descriptions must be accurate. For example a pair of leather shoes should be made of leather and not plastic and a computer advertised as including certain types of software already installed must not be supplied without the software. A box of chocolates described as containing 400 grams of chocolates must contain at least this weight of chocolates.

- All advertising must be accurate and provide correct information. For example a travel agent cannot state that a particular hotel is 'near the beach' if it is a twenty-minute drive from the sea.

- All goods (for example, electrical goods and toys for young children) must be safe and not cause injury or harm. For example, electrical equipment must not cause electrical shock and toys for small children must not contain parts which can be removed and swallowed. Chocolates should not be sold past their 'use by date'.

The legal framework (3): consumer protection

If goods are supplied that do not meet these requirements then the consumer can ask for a replacement or return the goods and have their money refunded. If services are supplied that are of a poor quality the supplier may be required to do additional (unpaid) work to bring the service up to standard.

In addition there is special protection for goods bought by telephone, by post, by digital TV or online.

- The consumer should receive clear information about the goods and services before deciding whether to buy them. This should include a description of the product, its price, the delivery time and any delivery charges.
- This information should be confirmed by the seller in writing.
- The consumer can change their mind and cancel the purchase for up to seven working days after buying the product.
- The supplier must have in place measures designed to minimise the risk of credit card fraud.

If a consumer feels that the product that has been supplied does not meet any of these legal requirements they should ask the supplier to correct any problems. If this does not solve the problem, the supplier can ultimately be taken to court and asked to pay compensation to the customer.

Implications for business

It can be argued that these laws simply require suppliers to adopt fair and honest practices when supplying goods and services. However, there are so many regulations and laws to be followed that it can be time-consuming to learn all about them and then put them into practice. This can be a particular problem for new, small businesses. The cost of putting right any problems can also be expensive, especially as this can include the cost of legal action taken by customers who feel a law has been broken.

> You can find out more about consumer protection by visiting the UK government website at www.berr.gov.uk/whatwedo/consumers/ index.html.

Tasks

1. A consumer buys a mobile phone that has a digital camera installed on it, but when they take it home they find that the digital camera is faulty. Describe how the supplier has broken the law and what the customer should do.

2. A business supplies luxury chocolates by post. What actions should the business take to ensure that it does not break any consumer protection laws?

3. Visit the website of an online retailer such as Amazon, Argos or Pets at Home. Find out how they implement UK consumer protection legislation (for example by studying their policy for returning goods). Present what you have found to your classmates.

4. Produce an information leaflet for consumers to help them understand their rights under consumer protection law.

5. Explain the benefits and drawbacks to a business of not following consumer protection laws. Do you think that businesses should do this? Give reasons for your answer.

Topic 1.14

The legal framework (4): data protection and access to information

Aims

By the end of this topic you should be able to:
- describe the principles of data protection and information access legislation
- analyse the actions required of business organisations in order to comply with data protection and information access legislation
- evaluate the impact on business organisations of the need to comply with data protection and information access legislation.

Do you know how many different organisations hold information about you? If you own a mobile phone, have a library card or have taken part in a survey at your local cinema you will have given your *personal information* to an organisation. Personal information is anything that can be used to identify you, for example your name or address.

> Write a list of the organisations that hold personal information about you.
>
> Create some rules that you would like these organisations to follow when storing or using your personal information.

Organisations that store and use personal information have to follow the *Data Protection Act*. This law helps to protect individuals' personal information by placing limits on what organisations can do with it. The Data Protection Act also sets out rules which organisations must follow when storing personal data. Finally, the Act gives individuals the right to view their personal data.

The Data Protection Act covers all personal data, whether it is stored on a computer or other media such as paper or video. The Act is enforced by a government regulator called the *Information Commissioner*. People who have their personal data stored by organisations are known as *data subjects*.

> Visit the Information Commission's website at www.ico.gov.uk to find out more about the Data Protection Act and keeping personal information safe.

Data protection principles

The Data Protection Act contains eight principles which organisations must follow if they collect personal data. The table on the next page summarises them.

The rights of data subjects

The Data Protection Act also gives data subjects the right to view their personal data. Organisations must allow this as long as the following conditions are met:

- The data subject makes a written request.
- The data subject can prove their identity.

The legal framework (4): data protection and access to information

Information must be:	What this means:
Fairly and lawfully processed	Data subjects should be told who will be processing their data and why. The data should not be used for any illegal purpose.
Processed for limited purposes	Organisations must only use the data for the specific reasons that were stated when it was collected.
Adequate, relevant and not excessive	Irrelevant information must not be collected.
Accurate and up-to-date	Organisations must ensure data is correct and if it isn't they must change it.
Not kept for longer than is necessary	Data that is no longer needed must be deleted.
Processed in line with your rights	If you change your mind about the organisation using your data it must comply.
Secure	Data should not be made available to unauthorised users, this includes data stored on laptops and storage disks.
Not transferred to other countries without adequate protection	Data should not be transferred to other countries, unless they have similar levels of data protection to the UK. All countries in the European Union (EU) have this level of protection so data can be lawfully transferred within the EU.

Principles that must be followed when collecting data

- A fee is paid if required by the organisation (usually £10 but it can be up to £50 if all data is paper-based and hard to find).
- The rights of other data subjects are not broken (this might happen if, for example, your data appears on a page that also contains other data subjects' personal information).

Organisations have to provide the requested data in a reasonable amount of time, up to a maximum of 40 days.

The other rights of data subjects are:

- the right to change any inaccurate personal data
- the right to prevent data being used for direct marketing (e.g. telephone calls and mail shots/junk-mail)
- the right to prevent data being used in ways that cause distress to the data subject.

Exemptions

Some data collected by the government is not covered by the Data Protection Act. This includes some data used by the police and the armed forces. The Data Protection Act only applies to personal data concerning the data subject. It cannot be used to obtain information, for example about a friend or work-colleague.

The impact of the Data Protection Act on business organisations

Complying with the Data Protection Act can be expensive for organisations. They have to make sure that all their systems meet the terms of the Act and if not, change them. For example, in February 2008 Marks and Spencer PLC was ordered by the Information Commissioner to make sure that all personal data stored on the company's laptops was encrypted. Doing this will have cost the business many thousands of pounds. Many large organisations employ full-time Data Protection Officers whose job is to help the organisation comply with the Act. On the other hand, all organisations in the UK are covered by the Act and so face similar costs.

In 2005 a new law came into force, the *Freedom of Information Act*. This law gives citizens of the UK the right to obtain information held by public bodies such as the government and local councils. The information can be on any subject; for example, an individual who objects to a supermarket building a new store in their town can request to see all the documents that the local council used to make its decision. The council has the right to refuse to give the information, but it must have a good reason and the applicant can appeal against the refusal to the Information Commissioner.

Tasks

1. Which of the following are items of personal information according to the definition used in this topic?
   a Your full name.
   b Your full address (including your postcode).
   c Your postcode (without the rest of your postal address).
   d Your passport number.
   e Your school or college.

2. Which of the following is NOT a Data Protection Act principle?
   a Information must be kept secure.
   b Information must be accurate and up to date.
   c Once given, information must not be changed or deleted.

3. You work as the Data Protection Officer for mp3Heaven, an online digital music store. You are told that a customer has arrived in the firm's reception area demanding to see all her personal data immediately. Under what circumstances can she see her data?

4. mp3Heaven does not yet have a data protection policy. Use a search engine to find the data protection policies of some business organisations and use them to create a short policy for mp3Heaven.

5. A supermarket receives a request to provide documents to a local resident about its 24-hour opening policy. Does the supermarket have to provide this information? Explain your answer.

Topic 1.15

The legal framework (5): copyright and computer misuse

> **Aims**
>
> By the end of this topic you should be able to:
> - describe the main principles of copyright and computer misuse legislation
> - analyse the actions required of business organisations in order to comply with copyright and computer misuse legislation
> - evaluate the impact on business organisations of the need to comply with copyright and computer misuse legislation.

We saw in the previous topic how the Data Protection Act places limitations on how organisations can use personal data. This includes the requirement to store data securely and to protect it from unauthorised use. In addition, there are laws which limit the actions that individuals can take to carry out unauthorised computer and data use.

Copyright, Designs and Patents Act

Anyone who creates an original piece of work, such as a report, a song, a digital photograph or a website has the right to claim ownership of the object and to place restrictions on its use by other people. This is called *copyright* and is designed to prevent the unauthorised copying or using of the work by someone else who then claims it as their own. For example, the text in this book is copyrighted which means it is against the law to copy the text without permission, for example by including the text in another book which is then sold for profit.

The Copyright, Designs and Patents Act (1988) is the main law in the UK which protects copyright holders, and it also applies to copyright material stored on computers and accessible via the internet. Some of the things which are illegal under the Act include:

- making an unauthorised copy of copyrighted computer data such as a computer program, a video clip, a piece of music or an image found on a website
- copying and pasting text from a copyrighted source without permission
- making small changes to a copied item of text or an image (e.g. by cropping it or changing colours) and claiming it as your own work.

Anyone seeking to use copyrighted material must seek permission from the copyright holder. They might be required to pay a fee in order to use it. Unfortunately, it is not always obvious who the copyright holder is. For example, you might wish to use a photograph of a pop star that you find on their official website. The copyright of the photograph might belong to the website owner, the pop star or even the photographer.

However, the Act states some activities that are allowed such as:

- using copyrighted materials for educational purposes (providing the copyright owner is acknowledged, e.g. by including a bibliography)
- making a single copy of a computer program for *back-up* purposes only.

In addition, some computer software manufacturers give permission for the user to install a piece of software on more than one machine, for example a home computer and a single laptop computer as well.

Software audits

Businesses are responsible for all the data stored on their computers. As a result many businesses regularly check their computers and network to make sure that they are not using unauthorised computer software. These checks are called a *software audit* which is made up of the following steps:

1. Identify all the software which the business has purchased.

2. Identify the licence requirements of the software (e.g. the number of computers the software can be installed on).

3. Check each computer and list the software installed.

4. Match the software installed with the licences held.

5. If there is any software installed without a licence then either:
   a delete the software or
   b purchase additional licences.

Breaking the Act

Computer users found guilty of breaking this law can face a demand for compensation by the copyright holder and, if taken to court and found guilty, an unlimited fine.

Computer Misuse Act

The Computer Misuse Act was introduced in 1990 in response to the growing problem of unauthorised access to computers in order to cause deliberate damage or harm. These problems grew as more and more computers were connected to the internet. The main areas made illegal under this act are:

- gaining access to a computer or network of computers without permission (this unauthorised use of computers is also known as hacking). Examples include logging on using someone else's user name and password or using knowledge of a computer system to bypass its security measures

- gaining unauthorised access to a computer with the intention of committing a crime (e.g. using customers' personal and credit card data stored on a computer to commit fraud)

- making unauthorised changes to a computer system (this includes editing or deleting data, or installing computer viruses).

Anyone found guilty of committing the first crime faces a six-month prison sentence and a maximum £2,000 fine. The second and last crimes each carry a penalty of up to five years in prison and an unlimited fine.

The legal framework (5): copyright and computer misuse

Tasks

1 Explain what is meant by the term 'copyright'.

2 For each of the following examples, state which of the two acts has been broken (some may break both acts!).
   a The text from a website is copied without permission and used in a book which is sold to the public.
   b The music on a CD is copied without permission and made available for others to freely download without paying for it.
   c A programmer creates a computer virus which is hidden inside an image on a website. Anyone downloading the image automatically installs the virus on their computer.
   d A program which automatically creates random passwords is used to gain access to a bank's computer system.
   e A friend gives you a copy of a computer program they have bought and invites you to install it on your home computer.
   f An employee hacks into the personnel files held on the computer network and increases their salary by £1000.

3 You wish to use a copy of a football team's logo as part of your school project. Explain what you should do if you wish to do this legally.

4 Produce an information leaflet that could be used in your school or college to inform computer users about the laws covered in this topic and what the users can and cannot do.

5 Explain how business organisations such as schools are affected by the two laws covered in this topic.

Topic 1.16

The legal framework (6): environmental protection

Aims

By the end of this topic you should be able to:
- describe the main principles of environmental protection legislation
- analyse the actions required of business organisations in order to to comply with environmental protection legislation
- evaluate the impact on business organisations of the need to comply with environmental protection legislation
- evaluate ways in which business organisations can act in a sustainable manner.

Environmental protection – the role of business

There are many reasons why businesses are being encouraged to do more to limit their impact on the environment. One of them is concern about the amount of waste thrown away each year and buried in *landfill sites*. Another is the threat posed by global warming. As a result, governments are requiring businesses to take action to reduce the amount of waste they produce, and to encourage them to recycle the waste they do produce.

Sustainable development

Sustainable development can be defined as the ability of the present generation on the planet to enjoy a quality of life that does not cause problems for future generations. Governments around the world are attempting to move towards this goal by, among other things, persuading businesses to minimise the impact of their activity on the environment. One example of how the government is trying to do this is the WEEE regulations.

The WEEE directive

In 2003 all fifteen member countries of the European Community (of which Britain is one) agreed to implement a set of rules called the Directive on Waste Electrical and Electronic Equipment (WEEE).

The WEEE regulations require manufacturers and suppliers of electrical and electronic equipment (e.g. mobile phones, printers, computers, televisions etc.) to take responsibility for their safe disposal when they reach the end of their useful life. This means producers have to pay for their products to be collected from customers and either recycled or safely disposed of.

The intention is that producers will try to save money by either designing products that last longer, or contain more parts which can be reused. In this way the impact of these products on the environment can be reduced.

> You can find out more about WEEE by visiting the government website: http://www.berr.gov.uk/whatwedo/sectors/sustainability/weee/page30269.html.
>
> Try visiting the website of an online retailer, such as Amazon, to find out how they implement this law.

The legal framework (6): environmental protection

For consumers of electrical and electronic equipment (including business users) this means that the producer will either take back the product at the end of its life or else the consumer can recycle it. The cost of this will be borne by the producer (though they can pass this on to the consumer, for example by charging them a higher price when they buy the product).

Other regulations

Packaging and Packaging Waste

The government requires all businesses to think carefully about the amount of packaging they use. Products should be enclosed in the minimum amount of packaging needed to make sure the product is transported safely and in good condition. In addition, producers are required to pay a contribution towards the cost of recycling packaging in the UK.

End of life vehicles regulations

This aims to reduce the amount of waste from cars and vans when they are scrapped by their final owner. In particular the last owner must be able to dispose of their vehicle free of charge (with the costs borne by the car's producer). The regulations also set targets for how much of a car must be reused or recycled to make new cars and restricts the use of hazardous substances in both new vehicles and replacement vehicle parts.

Implications for business

Manufacturers are likely to face higher costs as a result of these regulations. They will have to pay both for the recovery of their products from consumers but will also be expected to pay for their disposal and, wherever possible, their reuse in new products. Producers will attempt to pass on these higher costs to consumers, in the form of higher prices. Consumers (including households and businesses) will find it easier to dispose of their unwanted products, but they will be encouraged to use them for longer than they have done in the past.

Tasks

1 State two reasons why businesses are being required to reduce their impact on the environment.

2 Explain, in your own words, what is meant by the term 'sustainable development'.

3 You have just purchased a new computer. Explain how the environmental regulations described in this topic will affect the product you have purchased and how you will dispose of it.

4 Jackson Grange Limited manufactures clocks which it delivers by post throughout the UK. Produce an information leaflet describing how the business will be affected by environmental protection legislation.

Topic 1.17

Ethics and social responsibility

> **Aims**
>
> By the end of this topic you should be able to:
> - describe ways in which businesses can act in an ethical and socially responsible way
> - evaluate the impact on business organisations of acting (and not acting) in an ethical and socially responsible way.

Is it acceptable for businesses to employ children to make their products? Should businesses be prevented from polluting the environment? Should businesses be free to do whatever they want or should society place restrictions on how they operate?

These are all examples of ethical and social issues.

Business ethics

Ethics are the moral principles that help to decide whether something is right or wrong. These principles can change over time. For example in the UK, it was once considered acceptable that British-owned farms in places such as the Caribbean could use slave labour to grow their crops. Gradually, over time this view was challenged until, in 1833, slavery was abolished throughout the British Empire. In a similar way, the employment of children to produce manufactured goods, which was abolished in the UK over a hundred years ago, is becoming a growing issue today as people in richer countries object to the use of child labour in some poorer countries.

> Do you think that no business should ever be allowed to employ children under the age of 12? Why?

Business ethics are the principles that govern how businesses should, and actually do operate. Many businesses publish statements of their *ethical principles* – guidelines for how the business should and shouldn't behave towards customers, employees and the wider communities affected by its actions.

Social responsibility

Many business organisations aim to act in a responsible way towards those affected by their actions. *Corporate social responsibility* is the term used to describe the practice of operating in a responsible way. Examples of socially responsible business behaviour include the following:

- Investing in local communities, for example by sponsoring local organisations such as sports teams, or by supporting schools providing work experience placements and support for business courses.

- Working with local communities, for example by promoting equal opportunities.

- Responsible advertising, e.g. not producing advertisements that are, in part, designed to persuade under-age consumers to buy the firm's products.

- Designing and using products which reduce pollution and other environmental problems.

- Good employment practices, for example by helping staff to obtain new qualifications and take time off when they have family commitments.

Impact of ethics and social responsibility on business organisations

It is quite likely that operating in an ethical and socially responsible way will be more expensive for a business. For example, it costs money to sponsor a local football team. In addition, it takes up employee time to develop and then monitor ethical policies. Many large businesses employ full-time ethical and social responsibility officers to look at how the business can improve its behaviour. On the other hand, it can be argued that there are business benefits, for example sponsorship is a way of gaining publicity, and many customers would prefer to buy from a business which has a good public image. Indeed, some people argue that businesses only operate in a socially responsible way because it would be harmful to them if they didn't! In other words, it may simply be in businesses' interests to act in an ethical way.

The role of business in society

The debate about ethical and social responsibility is part of a much bigger question: what should the role be of business in the modern world? Some people argue that businesses should exist purely to make a profit for their owners. They believe that businesses should not be required to act in any particular way, or be subject to lots of laws and regulations. If people dislike what a business does then that business will lose customers and so be forced to change or close. Other people believe that businesses have a major responsibility to the people who are affected by their actions. They believe that businesses should be made to act in even more socially responsible ways than they are at present. What do you think?

Tasks

1. Which of the following is a correct definition of business ethics?
   a The principles which help to determine whether a business action is good or bad.
   b A business action which is of benefit to society.

2. Investigate a local business organisation. In what ways does it operate in a socially responsible way? Recommend some ways in which it can become even more socially responsible. What do you think will be the impact of these changes on the way the business is organised and how it will operate?

3. Produce a two-minute presentation entitled: What I think the role of a business should be in 21st century Britain. Present it to your class. Be prepared to defend your views from others who may disagree with you.

Section 1B: Introduction to communication systems

Topic 1.18

❯ Procedures for checking internal and external business communications

Aims

By the end of this topic you should be able to:
- **check business documents for errors and correct them**
- **assess the benefits and drawbacks of checking business communications for errors**
- **assess the impact on business organisations of a failure in communication.**

This book is mainly about the ways that businesses communicate with their employees, customers and others, and the systems they use to do this. Sometimes these communications will be verbal (for example in face-to-face discussions with potential customers or over the telephone), sometimes using text (for example when sending a letter to a customer or describing a product's features on a website) or sometimes visual (for example a poster or television advert). Businesses try to make sure these messages are accurate and leave a good impression on the customer, but what happens when mistakes are made? In this topic we will look at the consequences for the business if the communications it sends out contain errors, and what the business can do to ensure they are of a high quality.

Common errors

Factual errors

Sometimes mistakes are made because incorrect information is given out. For example a mobile phone could be described in a leaflet as having a battery which enables 220 minutes of talk time when the most that the battery can deliver is 120 minutes. A website might list the selling price of a computer game as being £29.99 when the actual price should be £39.99. Another mistake is to use an incorrect name when sending a letter to a customer. For example a letter intended for Mr Alex Browne might be mistakenly addressed to Mrs Alex Brown.

Errors of tone and message

In 2008 a group of elderly people living in a rest home received a letter from their local council telling them to stop feeding birds from their windows or face being sent to prison and losing their home. The council later apologised for the tone of the letter and agreed that it should have been more carefully worded.

Spelling and punctuation errors

Even if the facts are accurate and the tone of the message is appropriate, there can still be errors of spelling and punctuation. Common mistakes include incorrectly spelt words or using homonyms (words such as *their* and *there* which sound the same but have different meanings). Common punctuation errors include failing to use speech marks or using an exclamation mark too often!!!

Consequences of poor business communication

The problems caused by poor communication are many, but their impact on the business will depend on different factors, including how many people received the message and what was wrong with it. Some consequences are:

- loss of public confidence. A single mistake on a letter may not be noticed by many people. For others it is an annoyance. Only a small minority are likely to lose confidence in the business and go elsewhere. However, the more mistakes a business makes, and the more serious they are, the more likely customers are going to use a competitor

- cost of correcting the message. A business might spend thousands of pounds creating and printing a set of brochures for a new product only to discover the document contains many mistakes. A decision to reprint the brochure after correcting the mistakes could be very expensive

- costs of publishing an incorrect selling price. If a business advertises its products at an incorrect price which is too low it is *not* legally required to sell them at that price. This however is likely to give the customer a poor opinion of the business and they may then decide not to buy the product at the correct price. In 1999 Argos incorrectly advertised a television set as being for sale at £3. When the business realised it had made a mistake it corrected the price and cancelled the orders it had received. Publishing an incorrect price is illegal in the UK under the Consumer Protection Act of 1987 and shops can be fined up to £5,000 for each customer who has been misled.

Procedures for improving communications

The main method businesses can use to prevent mistakes is to have messages checked before they are sent out. This usually involves another person reading your communications before they are sent out. The reader will correct any mistakes and make suggestions for how the message can be improved. More important communications will usually be checked by several different people. Often these people will have different views as to what can and cannot be said, and the best way to say it. Checking for errors can slow down the process of sending out communications. It will also make it more expensive to create the messages, thus increasing business costs.

Tasks

1. Describe three different types of errors that could appear in a letter sent by a business to a customer.

2. Read the following text, taken from a business website, and correct any errors you find.

   We are famous for the high qualty of our buisness comunications. All hour communications are carefully checked bye a team of proof reeders, You can bee confedent that all our products are of an equally high standerd. This includes our new spots car. which will only cost yew £200.00!!

3. A sweet shop displays a chocolate bar for sale at 35p when the correct price should be 38p. Explain the problems this could cause the business. How serious do you think these problems are for the shop? Give reasons for your answer.

4 A mail order business posts out a catalogue to over 100,000 customers. The business then discovers that some of the prices are incorrect and product descriptions are inaccurate. The order form incorrectly gives the name and address of a competitor business to post the order to.
   a Describe what the business will have to do in order to correct these mistakes.
   b Explain the impact that this failure of communications is likely to have on the business.

5 Explain the benefits and drawbacks to a business of putting in place measures to improve the quality of business communications. Do you think businesses should put these measures in place? Give reasons for your judgement.

Topic 1.19

Manual and computer-based systems (1): manual systems

Aims

By the end of this topic you should be able to:
- describe the main features of manual and computer-based systems
- evaluate the usefulness of manual and computer-based systems.

How much paperwork do you produce in a year? How many exercise books and how much filing paper? Multiply this by every person at your school or college. Imagine that it all had to be stored in one place and you were responsible for organising it and keeping it safe. How would you do it?

In the days before computers became commonplace, all business documents were created on paper. Some studies even suggest that, as a direct result of computers and email, *more* paper is now being used by businesses than ever before.

Manual systems defined

A manual system uses a hard or permanent *storage media* such as paper. Documents are typically stored in filing cabinets, or in boxes on shelves. A visit to a large city-centre reference library will give you a good idea of what a large manual filing system looks like.

Usually, a filing system is divided into two parts: current storage and archive storage. As the name suggests, current storage involves keeping documents that are normally in use, or may be needed quickly, accessible to users. Archive storage involves keeping rarely used or old documents in a separate place, perhaps in a basement or even in a different building. Sometimes, to save space, archive materials are converted to a non-paper format such as microfilm. This involves photographing the paper document and shrinking the resulting image to as much as one-twentieth of the original size. In this way a large volume of paper can be converted to a relatively small amount of photographic film. A drawback of this method is the cost, including the cost of using special microfilm readers.

A microfilm reader

Methods of organising a manual filing system

A manual system involves the storage of large volumes of paper-based information. The system needs to have an efficient method of *storing* the information so that it becomes easier to *retrieve* a particular item when needed. The most common storage methods include:

- Alphabetical order: for example a customer service department could store letters received from customers by alphabetical order of surname. All that would be needed to retrieve the letter would be the name of the customer.

> Why would you need to know the full name of a customer in order to be sure you retrieve the correct letter?

- Chronological order: the same organisation could store letters by date sent or received. In order to retrieve a particular letter you would need to know the date when it was sent.
- Classification: documents could be stored according to the topic they are mainly about. A well-known example is the Dewey Decimal System used to store books in a library.

A problem with this method is that paper documents can only be stored using one method, but sometimes people might want to locate an item using a different piece of information. In order to solve this problem, manual systems often make use of an indexing system. The system will have different sets of index cards, each one stored according to a different category of information. For example, the letter-storage system described above might file the actual letters in the order they were created: the first letter is given a location code number of 1, the second 2, the third 3 and so on. In order to find the letters the system will have three index cards for each letter. One lists the date first, the second lists the name of the customer at the top and the third gives the subject. If someone doesn't know the name of the customer but knows when it was sent then they can search through the 'date' cards. If they know the subject but not the date, they can search the subject cards until they find the name of the person. Each card will also list the location code, and that can be used to find the letter.

Benefits and drawbacks

The main benefits of manual filing systems are:

- it is easier to control access to a manual system as people have to physically visit the location where the documents are stored. The documents can be archived in a separate room and brought to the reader by a librarian or archivist
- manual documents are generally long-lasting, especially if converted to a different form such as microfilm.

The main drawbacks of manual filing systems are:

- compared with computerised systems, they take up a large amount of space
- usually, only one copy of any document is stored, although back-up copies might be stored using microfilm. This makes it difficult for more than one person to use the same documents at the same time
- there is a risk of damage to the documents e.g. by accidentally tearing paper or damage caused by fire or flooding
- a reader has to visit the archive to view documents, or the documents have to be posted which carries a risk of loss or damage
- once removed, a document has to be returned to its correct location, otherwise it will be difficult to locate and retrieve it again.

Tasks

1. State three features of a manual filing system.

2. How is the storage of paper-based documents organised in your classroom? Describe the benefits and drawbacks of this system.

3. Devise a card index system to store and efficiently retrieve three items of information about each person in your class (you don't need to collect the information, just decide what information the system will store).

4. Describe the benefits and drawbacks of a library which has only one copy of each book it owns.

Topic 1.20

Manual and computer-based systems (2): computer-based systems

Aims

By the end of this topic you should be able to:
- **describe the main features of computer-based systems**
- **evaluate the usefulness of computer-based systems**
- **compare manual and computer-based systems.**

Most business organisations, apart from very small ones, now use computers to organise and store much of the information they generate. This is usually a consequence of the information having been created by computer in the first place. Most businesses organise their computers into networks of connected machines where most of the data is stored on a central computer, a *server*, before being distributed to the computers which need it, using either cables or a wireless transmitter. In later topics in this section you will study how these computer systems are organised, what they consist of and how they store information.

Benefits of computer-based filing systems

- More than one user can access the same information at the same time. This is especially true where groups of computers are joined together in a *network*.
- It is easier to make copies of documents. Once created, it is relatively easy to make copies of computer files. These *back-up copies* of data mean it is less likely that information will be lost.
- Less storage space is needed. Computers take up less space than filing cabinets full of paper documents. A single modern desktop computer could easily store the equivalent of over twenty *million* letters. That number of paper-based letters would require many hundreds of filing cabinets.
- It is quicker to search for documents. A computer is much faster than a human at searching through documents in order to find the correct item.
- Documents can easily be edited to create new ones. For example, a business could send an almost identical letter to many thousands of different customers, simply by inserting a different name and address into each one.
- Documents can be viewed remotely. Thanks to the internet, a computer user can be connected to a business network even though they are many hundreds of miles from where the business network is located.

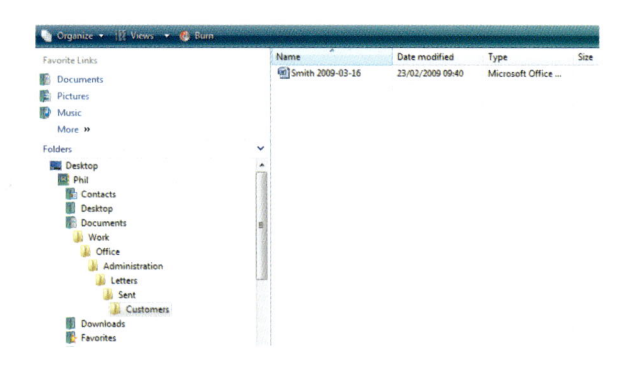

A computer-based filing system

Drawbacks of computer-based filing systems

- It is easy to delete or edit computer data. However it is possible to put in place security systems which make this difficult.
- Need for security systems. As well as preventing accidental deletion of data, computer systems are vulnerable to being accessed by unauthorised users. This is especially true of computer networks that operate over the internet.
- Cost of maintaining the network and training users. Computer systems are complex and are sometimes difficult to use. Businesses need to employ *network managers* to look after the network and run its security systems and network users may require training in how to use the system.
- It can be easier to locate information. This, however, depends on how well the system has been designed and the way in which computer files are stored. You might wish to ask yourself how easy it is to locate a specific file you have saved onto your school network or home computer. At the very least, files should be organised into folders and given filenames which describe the contents of the file.

Comparing manual and computer-based filing systems

More and more businesses are moving towards computer-based filing and storage systems. This is partly because of their benefits when compared to the problems of paper-based systems, but it is also a consequence of the increasing use of computers that creates the information in the first place. For example, most businesses use computers to generate letters which are then either printed and posted, or emailed to customers, so it makes sense to store them on a computer as well. In reality both methods of data storage are likely to be used by business organisations in future, if only because businesses continue to generate, send and receive paper-based communications as well as computer-based ones.

Tasks

1. What is a computer network?
2. Which is the better filename: 'Letter to Peter Jones' or '2008-07-14 Letter Jones Peter'? Give reasons for your answer.
3. Create a short presentation explaining how a small business such as a bookshop could set up a computerised filing system to replace its existing paper-based system.
4. Your school is planning to replace all paper-based filing systems with computer-based ones. What would be the benefits and drawbacks to your school/college of doing this? Overall, do you think this is a good idea? Give reasons for your conclusion.

Topic 1.21

Input devices (1)

Aims

By the end of this topic you should be able to:
- describe the main features of input devices
- evaluate the usefulness of specified input devices in a given scenario.

Over the next few pages you will learn about the main parts of the ICT (Information and Communications Technology) based systems that businesses use to create and distribute their communications. You will already be familiar with some of this technology, but will learn how it is used by business organisations. In this unit we concentrate on *hardware* (the physical equipment that is connected together to form a computer system).

We begin by looking at *input devices*. These are the hardware items that are used to enter information into the computer system.

Keyboards

You are likely to be very familiar with using a computer keyboard. A keyboard has two main purposes:

- to enter *text* (for example when creating a letter)
- to input *commands* into the computer (for example by pressing the delete key).

Common computer keyboard shortcuts:

Keystroke	Action
Control and C	copies highlighted text onto the clipboard
Control and V	pastes clipboard contents into a document
Control and S	saves currently open document

Most computer keyboards are called QWERTY devices. This is taken from the letters on the top row of letters on the keyboard. The reason for this is that computer keyboards are based on *typewriter* keys; the principle used in their arrangement was the need to ensure that no key would be placed next to a key that it usually followed in a word. This makes QWERTY keyboards slow to use unless you have been trained how to *touch type* with all of your fingers without having to look at the keys. Untrained 'two-fingered' typists can enter an average of around thirty words per minute; a trained touch typist can type up to four times more quickly.

Originally, all keyboards were connected to the computer by a wire, along which electrical energy passed to power the keyboard as well as the signals that gave the computer its commands. More recently, battery-powered *wireless keyboards* have become more common. Other modern developments include *virtual keyboards* where an image of a keyboard is projected onto a flat surface and *foldable keyboards* where the keypad is contained on a soft plastic background which can be folded up when not needed.

Using a keyboard can cause *repetitive strain injury*. To help solve this problem, some keyboards have been designed to minimise the health risks of using a keyboard. These are called *ergonomically-designed* keyboards.

Other types of keyboard include concept keyboards. Instead of a conventional set of keys arranged in a QWERTY format there are a smaller number of buttons; each one enters a specific command into the computer (for example 'add this item to the order' or 'calculate total price'). Concept keyboards are more efficient because the user has fewer buttons to press and each one relates to a specific action they need to perform. They are typically found in shops, restaurants and hotels. However, this technology is currently being replaced by touch-screen devices (see below).

Touch-screen devices

Touch-screen devices combine the functions of a keyboard with a computer screen. Instead of entering commands on a separate keyboard the user enters them directly onto the screen. The screen displays a page containing a number of different *hotspots* and is able to identify where on the screen is being touched. When a particular hotspot is touched then the computer carries out the command attached to that hotspot. For example, in a museum you might see a screen that shows images of a number of different exhibits: when an image of an exhibit is touched the screen then displays more information on it.

Touch-screen devices are often used by businesses in situations where it would be difficult to use a keyboard, for example in dirty environments such as factories, which might cause a keyboard to stop working.

A touch-screen device

Mice

A mouse is a well-known *pointing-device* used to enter commands into the computer. The principle behind a mouse is very similar to a touch-screen device except that the mouse travels along a two dimensional flat surface, such as a desk, and the user enters commands by clicking a button on the mouse rather than touching the screen directly. Originally, all mice were connected to the computer using a wire, along which signals were sent. More recently there has been a growth in the use of battery-powered *wireless* mice.

Tasks

1 State two uses of a computer keyboard.

2 What is a QWERTY keyboard?

3 Describe one drawback of a QWERTY keyboard for most users.

4 Give one benefit of using an ergonomically-designed keyboard.

5 Describe in your own words how a touch-screen device works.

6 Design a touch-screen interface which could be used in a supermarket to help customers calculate the price of fruit and vegetables based on how much a particular item weighs.

7 When would you use a mouse, rather than a keyboard, when working at a computer?

Topic 1.22

Input devices (2)

Aims

By the end of this topic you should be able to:
- describe the main features of input devices
- evaluate the usefulness of specified input devices in a given scenario.

In this topic we look at some more input devices.

Joysticks

A joystick consists of a stick which sits inside a base unit. The stick can be rotated in any direction (to indicate a turn) and pushed outwards in that direction (to indicate motion in that direction). The joystick usually has a number of buttons on it which can be used to enter a command rather like a mouse button.

Joysticks have long been used by computer-game players to control the movement and actions in a game. However, their main uses in business include controlling the actions of an aircraft or other devices which move in three dimensions, such as cranes or driverless vehicles. They are also used by people whose physical disability makes it hard for them to use a mouse to control a computer.

Scanners

A scanner is used to convert an existing hard copy of a document or object into a digital image. The scanner works by passing a beam of light across the surface of the document being scanned and uses the light reflected back from its surface to store a digital copy of the document.

There are many different types of scanner, but the most popular ones used by business include:

- flat-bed scanners: these are the ones you see in many homes and offices. They are designed for taking copies of documents and look like a small photocopier

- hand-held scanners: these are used in situations where a flat-bed scanner would be impractical. Examples include scanning *three-dimensional images* (e.g. a manufactured object) or for scanning in remote locations, such as when visiting a customer's home

- barcode scanners: these are generally used in shops, where a scanner reads a *barcode* which has been printed onto a product. The data

Joysticks can be used for different tasks

barcode is a visual representation of a series of numbers which when linked to a *product database* help to identify the product. For example, if the barcode printed on a can of baked beans is scanned at a supermarket checkout the product code is used to extract the price from a database and tell the database that one item has been sold.

- OCR: this stands for Optical Character Recognition software. OCR software can convert an image containing words into text on a computer. For example, it could be used to convert a paper copy of a customer letter into text which can be edited on a computer. OCR software is not yet 100% accurate.

Digital cameras

A digital camera creates a digital image of whatever the camera sees through its lens. Images can then be put onto a computer where they are stored and manipulated. A digital image is stored as a series of dots; each dot is called a 'pixel'. The more pixels there are, the more detailed the image will appear (think about how an image made up of just one pixel would look) – this is also known as the *resolution* of the image. Modern digital cameras typically take *high resolution* images containing several million pixels. A drawback is that the more pixels, the bigger will be the size of the computer file needed to store the image.

A *webcam* is a type of digital camera that captures moving images which can then be transmitted to other users across a network such as the *internet*.

Microphones

A microphone captures sound and converts it into either an electrical signal or, with a *digital microphone,* a stream of digital data which can be read by a computer. A microphone can be used together with *voice recognition software* to enable the computer to create text without the user entering it via a keyboard.

Voice recognition

Voice recognition (VR) software is used to convert spoken commands into text and commands which the computer recognises. It achieves the same results as a keyboard, without having to type. As such, it is often used by people who have a physical impairment which limits their ability to type. VR software takes the data collected by a microphone and compares it with a database of known words and phrases. Most VR software allows the user to improve its performance by 'training' it to recognise their own speech patterns.

VR software is used in other situations where voice commands are better than other forms of input. One example is to control some in-car *satellite navigation* systems where it would be dangerous to type text commands whilst driving.

The main drawback with VR software is that it is not yet 100% accurate.

Tasks

1. State two business situations where a joystick could be used to give commands to another device.

2. You wish to convert a letter from a customer into a digital image. Describe how you would do this.

3. Which has the bigger file size, a low-resolution or a high-resolution image?

4. What is a pixel?

5. Explain how somebody who has limited use of their hands can enter text using voice recognition software.

6. You have been asked to create a letter which is to be sent to a customer. You have been asked to take a photograph of the outside of the business and include this image in the letter. Explain which input devices you will use to produce this letter.

Topic 1.23
Output devices (1)

Aims

By the end of this topic you should be able to:
- describe the main features of output devices
- evaluate the usefulness of specified output devices in a given scenario.

An output device is anything which is used by the computer to communicate back to the user. Examples include monitors, printers and speakers.

Computer monitor

Monitors are also known as *visual display units* (VDUs). They are perhaps the most commonly used output device. A monitor gives a visual display of the information being created by the computer. A monitor is generally used whenever a permanent copy of the output is not needed. An example is creating a letter for a customer. A monitor will be used to display the letter whilst it is being created and changes are made to it. Once the letter is finished a permanent copy will be made by printing it onto paper.

There are three main types of VDU technology:

- Cathode Ray Tube (CRT). This is now quite an old technology and has largely been replaced by newer ones. CRT monitors are heavy and large, they can be as deep as they are wide. Benefits of a CRT monitor, however, are that they display high-quality images and are cheaper and more long lasting than the monitors which have replaced them.

- Plasma screen monitors trap a group of gases between two glass panels. Electrical signals are used to change the properties of the gas so it displays a visual image. The benefits of plasma displays are:
  - they have a very high-quality image which makes them ideal for large-screen displays in clubs, restaurants and office reception areas.
  - they have a long display life: the plasma screen itself has a design life of nearly thirty years (longer than the other components of the equipment are likely to last).

The main drawback of plasma displays is the cost.

As the technology improves, plasma monitors are gradually being replaced by LCD monitors.

- Liquid Crystal Display (LCD) monitors are the most popular ones currently used by business and households. LCD monitors (also known as Thin Film Transistor – TFT monitors) work by using electrical signals to light up individual dots (or pixels) on the monitor's surface. The greater the number of pixels, the higher the screen resolution.

The benefits of LCD monitors are:

- they are very thin, so take up less space on a desk or shelf

- they do not generate as much heat as a CRT monitor.

    However they also have drawbacks:

- they do not have as good a picture quality as CRT monitors

- the viewing angle is not as good as CRT monitors, meaning that the picture quality is lower when viewed from above or the side.

Data projectors

A data projector takes a video signal and projects it onto a surface using a lens and a bulb to create a strong beam of light. Data projectors have two main uses:

- to project slide show presentations onto a screen so that they can be seen by a large group of people in a room or lecture hall. Since they can be used to display any computer output they are often used in classrooms to help students learn how to use computer software

- as part of a home cinema system. Data projectors can be used as an alternative to more expensive large LCD or plasma screen monitors to view television or DVD movies.

Benefits of data projectors:
- better and cheaper than monitors for displaying very large-sized images
- portable, so can be carried between locations.

Drawbacks of data projectors:
- it can be very expensive to replace the bulb. Bulbs have a relatively short life, typically 2,000 hours
- it is dangerous to look directly into the data projector whilst it is operating as the strong beam can cause eyesight damage.
- they work best in darkened rooms, making them impracticable in certain daylight conditions.

Tasks

1. What do the following initials stand for: CRT, LCD, TFT?
2. Describe the main differences between the appearance of a CRT monitor and an LCD monitor.
3. Explain the benefits and drawbacks of using an LCD monitor.
4. A travel agency business uses CRT monitors in all of its shops. Explain the benefits and drawbacks of this for the business and its workers.
5. State three occasions where you might use a data projector.
6. You have been asked to give a presentation to your school assembly. Which technology listed on this page should you use to display the slides to your audience? Explain your answer.

Topic 1.24
Output devices (2)

Aims

By the end of this topic you should be able to:
- describe the main features of output devices
- evaluate the usefulness of specified output devices in a given scenario.

Printers

After monitors, perhaps the most used computer output device is a printer. A printer is used to create a permanent copy (also called *hard copy* or *paper copy*) of a document. There are several different types of printer. The most common ones used in business organisations are the following:

Inkjet printer

This is currently the most common type of printer used by business organisations and households. These printers work by spraying ink directly from a print head onto a sheet of paper. Most inkjet printers use black ink to create black and white images and use a combination of black ink together with blue (cyan) red/purple (magenta) and yellow inks to create colour images.

The main benefits of inkjet printers are:

- the printer technology itself is quite low-cost. So inkjet printers are fairly cheap to buy
- the print quality is good, making them suitable for printing high-quality colour documents and images.

The main drawbacks of inkjet printers are:

- they are relatively slow, making them unsuitable for printing large volumes of documents
- they use a lot of ink, which itself can be quite expensive, resulting in high *operating costs* – the cost of printing each page can be quite high
- having to wait for the ink to dry to avoid smudges.

Laser printer

Laser printers are generally used in preference to inkjet printers where speed is important. A laser is used to etch an image of the document to be printed onto a rotating drum. An electrical charge is then applied to the drum and this enables it to attract a special ink (called *toner*) which is then transferred onto a sheet of paper when it is rolled across the surface of the drum. Laser printers are more expensive to purchase than inkjets, but the cost per page is less; they can print faster than inkjets and the quality is higher.

Thermal printer

Thermal printers use a heater to raise the temperature of specific parts of heat-sensitive paper. When heated the paper turns black. In this way an image or text can be printed. The main benefits of thermal printers are that they are cheap and can print large volumes of small straightforward documents. Their main drawbacks are that the resulting document does not last very long before the image degrades and they are not suited to creating complex images. Their main use today is for printing receipts in unmanned locations, for example petrol stations.

Dot-matrix printer

This is an old technology which is fast being replaced. The ink is stored on a ribbon which is pressed against paper by a series of pins stored on a *print head*. Each pin creates a single printed dot on the page.

The main drawbacks are that the technology is very noisy and the print quality is limited by the number of dots which can be created. Also, the technology is not designed for colour printing.

The main benefits are the low cost of the printers (and the ink) and the fact that the pressure of the pins against the paper means that *multi-part stationery* can be used. This is where several sheets of paper are held together and each one has a layer of ink on the back; this means that whatever is printed on the top copy can be printed at the same time onto all other copies. This makes dot-matrix a useful technology for printing documents such as receipts, where the business and the customer both need copies of the same document.

However, the biggest drawback is the poor print quality (there are not enough dots on the print head to enable high-quality images, complex graphics or fonts to be printed) and this is the main reason why the technology has been largely replaced.

Speakers

Speakers are an increasingly common output device. They are normally used to display sounds such as music files, radio programmes or soundtracks to movies or presentations. They also still have a use for the computer to communicate *error messages* to the user. Speakers are also combined with *text to speech software* to enable the computer to give an audio output that is particularly useful to blind and partially sighted users.

Tasks

1 Describe briefly how each of the following types of printer work:
   a inkjet
   b laser
   c dot-matrix
   d thermal

2 State two benefits of using an inkjet printer.

3 State two drawbacks of using a dot-matrix printer.

4 Explain when you might use an inkjet printer in preference to a dot-matrix printer.

5 You have been asked to print ten copies of a four-page colour leaflet that includes photographs. Which type of printer would you use? Give reasons for your answer.

6 Modern offices usually use both inkjet and laser printers. Explain why both types of printer are needed.

7 Explain how a partially-sighted user could use speakers as part of their computer system.

Topic 1.25

Computing devices (1)

Aims

By the end of this topic you should be able to:
- **describe the main features of computing devices**
- **evaluate the usefulness of specified computing devices in a given scenario.**

In this topic we will look at computing devices – those that sit between input and output devices. A computing device is basically a piece of hardware that *processes* data by manipulating or changing the data which is input into it before then communicating the results back to the user via an output device.

Desktop computers

The main device used in business organisations are desktop computers. These can either be used as *standalone* machines or grouped together to form a *network*.

Desktop computer systems usually consist of the following devices connected together:

- input devices: mouse, keyboard, scanner
- output devices: monitor, printer
- the computer itself
- communication devices: e.g. a modem to connect to the internet.

Desktop computers need *software* in order to perform. There are two main types of software:

- Operating Systems software: this is needed to run the computer so that it is able to receive instructions and carry out its operations. Well-known operating systems include *Microsoft Windows* and *Macintosh OX*.
- Applications software: this is needed to perform specific tasks that benefit the user. For example *word processing software* is needed to create text-based documents and *browser software* is needed to view Webpages when using the internet.

A desktop computer

A computer usually contains the following main parts:

- Computer case: made of plastic or metal.
- Motherboard: containing all the most important components needed to make the computer work.
- Central Processing Unit (CPU): this performs all the calculations and decisions that the computer is required to carry out by the software.
- Main memory: this is where data is held whilst it is being used by the CPU. If the computer is suddenly switched off all this data will be lost.
- Long-term memory (also called the hard disk): this is where all software and data is stored until it is deleted.

- Video and sound cards: these enable the computer to display video images and play sound files.

Desktop computers are designed to operate as an individual unit. They contain all the hardware and software that enable them to do this. Sometimes however, computers are connected together to form a network. Most of the computers in your school or college are probably connected together to form a network. Each computer attached to a network is called a *workstation*. One computer, however, is likely to control the workings of the network and possibly store files which can be sent to any workstation: these computers are called *network fileservers*.

There are many benefits of using a computer network:

- it is possible to use any machine on a network. This means, for example, that employees do not always have to sit at the same desk
- files and programs can be stored in a central location and made available across the whole network. So, for example, you could create a file at one workstation and then edit it using a different one in another location on the network
- hardware can be shared by different network users. This can save the business money as fewer printers, scanners and other devices are needed.

There are also drawbacks:

- the network is at risk from unauthorised users. Network security is important, especially because of the growth of *wireless networks* where computers connect to the network by exchanging radio signals with a network server or a device called a network *router*. Technically, any computer can join a wireless network and so it is important to have measures in place to protect the network from unauthorised users. These measures are discussed in Topics 1.30, 1.31 and 1.32.
- if there is a problem with the network server then it is likely that the whole network will stop working.

Tasks

1. What is missing from the following computer system: input device, computer, communication device?
2. Name two types of application software.
3. Name one brand of operating system.
4. State four components of a standalone computer.
5. Describe three benefits to a business of connecting its computers together into a network.
6. Describe two drawbacks of operating a computer network.

Topic 1.26

Computing devices (2)

Aims

By the end of this topic you should be able to:
- describe the main features of computing devices
- evaluate the usefulness of specified computing devices in a given scenario.

Portable computers

Laptop computers

A laptop computer is a smaller version of a desktop computer. It is designed to be used in any location. The main differences between a desktop and a laptop computer are:

- laptops are smaller and lighter
- laptops have a built-in keyboard and screen
- laptops can be powered by mains electricity and a rechargeable battery.

The main advantage of a laptop computer is that it allows a worker to use a computer when away from their workplace. For example, a salesperson can use a laptop computer when staying in a hotel, travelling on a train or visiting a customer.

The main benefits of using a laptop are:

- laptops are portable, so they can be easily carried
- they are small so can fit inside briefcases or small backpacks
- they use the same operating systems and applications software as a desktop computer
- most have a *wireless internet* facility which means the user can send and receive emails and view web pages whilst away from the office
- they help make workers more *productive* because they are able to work whilst travelling or whenever they are away from the office.

The main drawbacks of using a laptop are:

- they are fragile, so can be easily damaged
- they can be lost or stolen, resulting in a loss of important data
- they are light enough to carry, but heavy enough to cause injury if, for example, the user has a poor back or does not carry the laptop correctly
- if one component such as the screen or keyboard becomes damaged then the whole laptop may have to be replaced
- laptops are less powerful than desktop computers, for example they may have a smaller *hard-drive* and so store fewer files
- laptops are more expensive than an equivalent desktop computer.

Netbooks

These are smaller and cheaper versions of laptops, designed specifically for use whilst travelling. Netbooks are generally smaller than laptops, have much less memory and are designed for web-browsing and general computing tasks such as word-processing.

Handheld computers

Handheld computers are smaller than laptops and are designed for situations where using a laptop would be impractical. The most common type of handheld device is a Personal Digital Assistant (PDA). A PDA is a very small personal computer that contains most of the features of larger computers, for example:

- input: information can be entered using a *stylus* to either write onto a screen (software is used to convert the writing to text) or to press characters on an on-screen keyboard. An inbuilt microphone captures voice messages
- output: information can be read from a small screen or listened to using headphones.

PDAs became popular during the beginning of the 21st Century; however the technology has been combined with mobile phones to create smartphones. These are mobile phones which also include the features of a PDA. Smartphones are replacing PDAs as the main handheld computing device.

A smartphone

Apart from mobile phone use, the main business uses for PDAs and smartphones are email and diary management. These devices also contain software that enables the user to *synchronise* the information on their PDA/smartphone with the email and diary management software on their desktop computer when they return to the office. In addition, these devices often contain spreadsheets, word-processing and database software so the user can read and edit documents whilst on the move.

The main benefits of handheld devices are:

- they are smaller than laptops so do not carry the health risks from carrying a heavier device
- they can be stored in a pocket
- they can be used anywhere as they are more flexible than a laptop.

Drawbacks of handheld devices are:

- being so small, they are easy to lose
- they are less powerful than laptop computers
- using a stylus can be fiddly – they are not designed for using for long periods or for editing complex documents.

> Studies have suggested that over 100,000 handheld devices are lost in London every year. Many of these devices contain sensitive business data.

Electronic point of sale (EPOS) devices

These devices are found in most shops and other places where a customer buys a product. They work in the following way:

- the cashier scans a *barcode* on a product using a *barcode reader*
- the barcode contains data which defines the product being sold. This data is used to connect to the business's stock and product databases
- the product database is used to display the price of each product being sold
- the EPOS device calculates the total cost of all the products bought by the customer and displays the total price
- the customer enters their *payment card* into the EPOS device's *card reader*

- the EPOS device checks with the customer's bank that the payment card is valid. If it is valid the customer is asked to authorise the payment by entering their personal identification number (PIN) using a keypad. If they enter the correct number then the payment is deducted from their bank account
- the quantity of sold items is deducted from the shop's stock database.

Tasks

1. State two differences between a laptop and a desktop computer.

2. State three benefits to a business of giving its salespeople laptop computers.

3. John Brown works two days a week in his office as an architect. He spends three days a week visiting customers who could be anywhere in the country. Explain how he could use portable computing devices in his job.

4. A business is considering replacing all its networked desktop computers with laptop computers which can connect to the network using a wireless connection. Explain the benefits and drawbacks of this for the business. Overall, do you think it is a good idea? Give reasons for your conclusion.

Topic 1.27
Storage devices (1)

Aims

By the end of this topic you should be able to:
- describe the main features of storage devices
- analyse the benefits and drawbacks of storage devices
- evaluate the usefulness of storage devices in a given scenario.

Computers exist to enable users to store and manipulate data. In this topic we will look at how this data can be stored. There are basically three locations where data can be stored:

- inside the computing device itself. An example is a *hard disk*
- on a *removable* medium which can be stored away from the computer by the user, e.g. a compact disc
- on a *remote* storage device which the user has no direct control over. An example is using the internet to transfer data to another organisation's storage system.

Hard disks (internal and external)

A hard disk is a circular magnetic disk. Data is stored using a read/write head which passes over the rotating surface of the disk and either reads the data stored or adds data to it. Most computers have a number of these disks placed on top of each other inside a sealed *hard disk drive* unit. The more disks are used, the greater the *storage capacity* of the hard disk drive. Almost all computers have at least one hard disk drive inside their main unit (called an *internal hard disk drive*). However, it is also possible to use an *external hard drive*. This can be connected to the computer to give either additional storage capacity or to create a *back-up* copy of the computer's data.

Hard disk drives have a large memory capacity, making them ideal as the main permanent storage facility in most computers. The read/write head can move at great speed, making it possible to locate a specific piece of data very quickly. However, the disks themselves are very fragile and can be damaged, for example if the read/write drive *crashes* and damages the surface of the disk. For this reason alone it is always a good idea to store a back-up copy of the data stored on a hard disk.

Magnetic tape

Magnetic tape was one of the earliest media developed to store computer data. It works in a similar way to a hard disk, the main difference being that the magnetic material is in a continuous ream of tape which is stored on a reel. The main benefit of magnetic tape is that it has a very large memory capacity at a cheaper price than other forms of data storage. The main drawback is that it takes a long time to locate a specific item of data on the tape, making it unsuitable for use as the main storage device whilst working with data. However, it is still used today by many organisations to store large volumes of back-up computer data.

Storage devices (1)

Portable flash drives (e.g. USB memory sticks and memory cards)

Flash memory works in a similar way to magnetic memory, the main difference being that the data is stored on a single computer chip and electricity is used to create the data. Flash memory devices generally have a smaller capacity than magnetic devices but the device itself is more robust, making it suitable for devices such as handheld computers or digital cameras, especially where data needs to be transferred between devices using a flash memory device.

The main flash memory devices are USB memory sticks. These small devices are about the size of a key-ring and contain a flash memory device. Cheaper devices have a smaller memory capacity than a CD but newer devices can have a capacity similar to a DVD. Their main use is to transfer data between computers.

A drawback with flash drives is that data can only be written to them a limited number of times. After this they will stop working, so they should not be used as the only memory device to store back-up copies of important data

Memory cards

These are the same as memory sticks, the only difference being that the data is stored on a card which can be inserted into a slot in a card reader. These readers are often installed on devices such as smartphones, digital cameras and printers designed to print photographs directly from a memory card.

The main benefits of flash devices are their small size and increasingly large memory capacity. This means they can be used to transfer large volumes of data. For example, a presenter may need to travel in order to deliver a slideshow presentation. They only need to take a memory stick containing the presentation file and then plug it into a computer at the venue. The main drawbacks are that flash devices are only able to have data written to them a limited number of times (up to 100,000) and they can be used to steal important data (for example by an employee copying data onto a memory stick before leaving to work for a competitor).

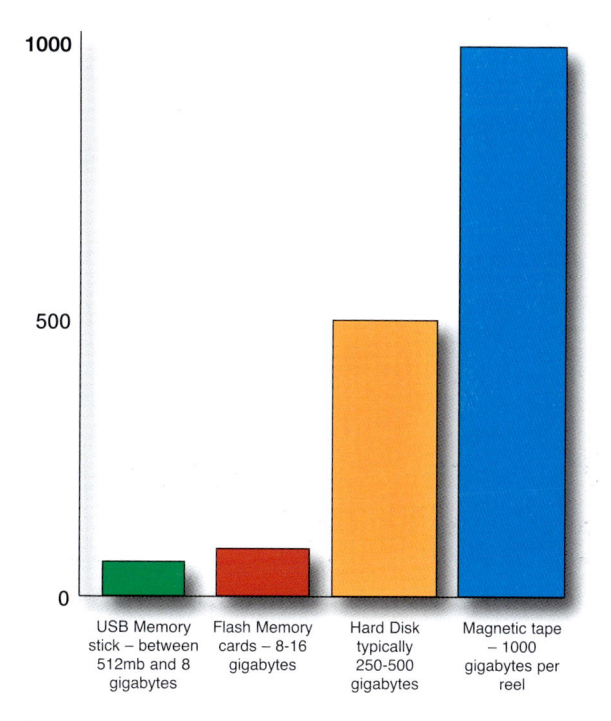

Chart of the memory capacity of different storage devices

- USB Memory stick – between 512mb and 8 gigabytes
- Flash Memory cards – 8-16 gigabytes
- Hard Disk typically 250-500 gigabytes
- Magnetic tape – 1000 gigabytes per reel

Tasks

1. Explain the difference between an internal and an external hard disk drive.
2. State one benefit and one drawback of storing data on an internal hard disk.
3. State one benefit and one drawback of storing data on an external hard disk.
4. Explain how you could make use of a USB memory stick.
5. Explain how a flash memory card could be used to transfer images between a digital camera and a desktop computer.
6. A business is considering issuing a USB memory device to every employee who uses its computer network. Explain the benefits and drawbacks to the business of doing this. Overall, do you think it is a good idea? Explain your conclusion.

Topic 1.28
Storage devices (2)

Aims

By the end of this topic you should be able to:
- Describe the main features of storage devices
- Analyse the benefits and drawbacks of storage devices
- Evaluate the usefulness of storage devices in a given scenario.

Optical disks

An optical disk is a flat circular disk where data is stored in pits or bumps on its surface. The disk is coated with a reflective material and the data is written or read by a read/write head. Because the disk and its data are more robust than magnetic or flash memory they can be handled directly by the user, but are usually stored inside a plastic case when not needed.

The main types of optical disk are Compact Disks (CD), Digital Versatile Disks (DVD) and newer technologies such as blu-ray. However, the basic differences between them are the technologies used to read and write data to them, and their storage capacity.

Compact discs

Compact Disk (CD) is an early type of optical disk. They were first used in the 1990s and have a maximum capacity of either 650 or 700 megabytes of data. This is enough for up to 80 minutes of music. CDs are generally used for music or computer programs sold by music and software producers. They are also used for storing small amounts of back-up data or for transferring files between users.

There are three main types of CD:

- CD-ROM (where ROM stands for Read Only Memory) – these are mass-produced to contain data which cannot be deleted or edited. As such they are used by manufacturers to supply software such as computer programs.
- CD-R (where R stands for Read) – these are usually sold blank and allow the user to 'burn' data to them which then cannot be removed. A training company might use CD-Rs to store files which it gives to delegates who attend its training sessions.
- CD-RW (where RW stands for Read and Write) – these are CDs where the user can add and then delete data. These are the most flexible, as well as being the most expensive type of CD to buy. However, the data written to them may not be viewable on all computer systems.

DVDs

DVDs were first developed in the 1990s. They work in a very similar way to Compact Disks but are able to store much greater volumes of data – a standard DVD holds 4.7 gigabytes of data (equivalent to more than six CDs). As a result DVDs are used to store high-quality movies of up to two hours. Like CDs, DVDs come in ROM, R, and RW versions. However, unlike CDs there are two main technologies: DVD+ and DVD- used to add data to the disks. This means that DVDs created by one computer are not always useable on other computers.

Newer technologies

Blu-ray disks have used improvements in the technology to store around ten times the amount of data on a standard DVD. Their original business use was for the distribution of *high-definition* movies.

Ultra Density Optical discs (UDO) have a storage capacity of over ten times that of a blu-ray disk.

Optical disks have the benefit that they are small and portable and can hold relatively large amounts of data. As a result they are used by some businesses to store back-up copies of data and for transferring files between users. A drawback of both is that this makes them vulnerable to theft. Large amounts of data can be stolen in this way. They also have the drawback that compared to magnetic and flash memory devices, optical devices can take a long time to have data written to them. Another problem is that each new type of disk technology cannot be used on older players and recorders. For example a DVD player cannot be used to play blu-ray disks.

Remote storage

Remote storage services have developed because it is possible to transfer data between different computers using the internet. They are mainly used for storing back-up copies of data; this is covered in the next topic.

One other use of remote storage is for *home-based workers* and other people who work using laptops. Often, the data used is transferred between the head office business computer and the user's laptop over the internet. This means that the data is not stored on the laptop but at the head office, so any loss or theft of the laptop does not result in important data being lost.

Tasks

1 What do the following initials stand for: CD, DVD, CD-ROM, DVD-R, CD-RW?

2 Why is it possible to remove an optical disk from its protective case?

3 Give one business use for each of the following devices:
- CD-ROM
- DVD-ROM
- CD-R
- DVD-RW.

4 A business wishes to use an optical disk to store two gigabytes of data. Should they use a CD or a DVD to store the data? Give a reason for your choice.

5 Explain when a business might make use of each of the following storage media:
- Internal hard-disk drive
- Magnetic tape
- USB memory stick
- CD-RW
- DVD.

Topic 1.29
Back-up systems

Aims

By the end of this topic you should be able to:
- describe how and why computer data should be backed up
- analyse the benefits and drawbacks of backing up computer data
- evaluate the effectiveness of back-up methods and systems in a given context.

Computers are very delicate machines: for example a laptop dropped onto a hard floor will almost certainly be damaged beyond repair. Unfortunately, one of the parts of a computer most likely to fail is the internal hard drive. It is possible to retrieve the data on a broken hard disk, but this can only be done by experts and is not always successful.

It is also possible to accidentally delete important files. Clicking the save button on an opened document immediately after having deleted a part of the text will result in a loss of information that then cannot be retrieved.

It is therefore vital for businesses that their important computer files are protected from the risk of loss or damage by making *back-up* copies of them.

A back-up file is a copy of a file that is used to replace the original if it is lost or damaged. Most organisations make back-ups of their computer data at regular intervals, perhaps once a week or, in the case of very important files, every day.

There are a number of issues which should be considered when deciding the best way to back up computer data.

What should be backed up?

The easiest way to back up data is to take a copy of a file or folder then save it in a different location such as a folder on a memory stick. This is the way that individuals can make a back-up copy of a document they have been working on. However, a business might also wish to make a back-up copy of its entire computer system: this will include software programs and operating system files.

How should data be backed up?

The basic decision is whether data should be backed up manually (e.g. by copying and pasting files) or by using an automated process (e.g. setting a schedule that data is backed up every Friday night). A problem with manual methods is that the user may forget. A problem with automated systems is that they are not always successful, so need to be checked for accuracy.

How often should back-up copies of data be made?

There are many factors affecting the frequency of back-ups, these include:

- how important is the data? The more important, the more frequent the back-up should be made

- how often are the data files changed? If a file is changed every day, then arguably, a back-up copy should be made each night

- how much will it cost the business if the data is lost? If the cost of replacing the data is very small, then it might not be worth the time and expense of keeping back-up copies

- how many back-up copies to keep? Most organisations aim to keep more than one back-up copy, and they will keep earlier copies for a period of time just in case there are problems with the more up-to-date copies.

The choice of back-up media

All of the media contained in Topics 1.27 and 1.28 could be used to store back-up copies of data. The key issues affecting which one(s) should be used are:

- the amount of data to be stored: small amounts of data could be stored on a CD, but magnetic tape might be needed for large amounts of data

- length of time needed: some media might last longer than others. For example the surface coating on optical disks fades after a time

- speed of writing: flash drives are much faster to write to than magnetic tape

- robustness of the media: hard disks are prone to failure whereas an optical disk, stored safely, should last a number of years

- security of storage: it is very easy to lose a small USB memory stick, much harder for a thief to carry away boxes of magnetic tape.

The location of back-up storage media (including remote storage)

The basic principle here is that the back-up data should be stored in a separate place to the original data, because a fire could easily destroy both if they are kept in the same place! The other main consideration should be the speed with which the back-up copy would be needed if there was a problem with the original data.

Ideally, the back-up data should be stored in a secure, locked and fire-proof location.

Remote storage services

A recent development has been the growth of businesses which provide back-up services to other businesses and individuals over the internet. The customer pays the back-up provider a fee and they then transfer a copy of their data over the internet and the back-up provider takes responsibility for keeping the data securely. Some individuals even use a web-based email account such as Yahoo or Google Mail to store data remotely.

This method has the benefit that the data is stored at a different location to the main data; it can also be retrieved from anywhere in the world. However there are a number of drawbacks which have to be taken into account:

- the customer needs to be sure that their data is secure whilst it is being transferred over the internet (we will look at this issue in the next topic)

- the customer should be happy with the storage media used by the back-up provider

- the customer needs to be able to trust the host to keep the data secure
- the customer should be aware that the back-up provider's business could fail, and that their data would be safe even if this happened.

Tasks

1 Zara Payne is the new network-manager for WebDreemz Ltd, a business which sells holidays over the internet. Zara does not believe that back-up copies should be made of computer data. In your own words, explain to Zara why it is important to her business that back-up copies of computer data should be made.

2 Julian Sandey runs a business that makes and sells wooden toys. Orders are received by post but Julian transfers customer information onto a computer in order to create a record of who he has sent toys to and how much he has been paid. He also uses his computer to store his designs as well as a digital photograph of each toy he has made. He typically receives orders for between 10 and 15 toys each week. At the moment Julian does not back up his computer files. Recommend a suitable back-up system for Julian. You should consider all of the issues covered in this topic.

3 Investigate how data is backed up at your school/college, or at a local business. What reasons are there for the methods used? Are there any recommendations you can make for how the back-up systems can be improved?

Topic 1.30
Data security (1)

Aims

By the end of this topic you should be able to:
- **describe the main measures available to protect computer systems**
- **evaluate the usefulness of protection measures in a given scenario.**

Just think about the data you have stored on your school's computer system: how much of that data would you be willing to let anyone else have access to, to do with as they please? The answer is probably: not a lot! Whilst it is OK for an authorised computer user to edit, copy and delete files, this is not something that just anyone should be able to do.

There are many different threats to computer systems and the data stored on them. These threats have increased considerably with the growth of computer networks and the internet. This topic looks at some of the most important threats and how computer systems can be protected from them.

Threats to computers and the data they hold

Hackers

Unless protected, anyone could potentially gain access to a computer system to edit, copy or delete computer files. Unauthorised users are sometimes called *hackers*.

Malware

Malware is the term for any computer program installed either deliberately or accidentally on a computer with the intention of causing harm. The most common types of malware are:

- viruses: these are programs designed to disrupt the workings of a computer. They are called viruses because they are designed to be spread from one infected machine to another. Viruses can be downloaded from websites or installed by opening a file attached to a SPAM email

- spyware: this is software designed to monitor the ways the computer is used and then report this back to someone. One example is *keystroke* software: this could be used to record someone's password being typed into a bank website

- adware: this is software designed to monitor your internet use and then display adverts based on your web-browsing habits. Some software producers include adware in their programs as a way of getting back some of the costs of developing their products. Many people believe that adware is an invasion of privacy

- phishing: this is when you receive an email pretending to be from your bank or other business, requesting that you visit their website and re-enter your password or other personal data. In reality, the website is a fake and the owner will use the data they collect from you to hack into your real bank account to withdraw money. Phishing emails are examples of SPAM.

SPAM is the email equivalent of junkmail. The sender will often send the same message to thousands of random email addresses. They are hoping that just a few people will respond. Often the email contains a fake offer to buy something. SPAM is a very common way of sending viruses. Some SPAM emails include an internet link at the bottom of the message which invites the reader to click in order to remove themselves from the mailing list. This is often just a way of confirming that the email address of the reader is a valid one. SPAM senders then often add this address to a list which they send to other spammers!

There are a number of solutions which can reduce the risks to computer data. Some of these are precautions which any user should take while some require software to be installed and used. Others are a feature of the design of the computers themselves and the buildings where they are kept.

User precautions against unauthorised access to files

Users should be very careful when using the internet and email. In particular:

- *never* open an email attachment unless you are certain what the file contains. This especially includes emails received from people you do not know (SPAM messages)

- be very careful when visiting websites – always be on the look out for potential problems

- *never* give out your personal data to sources unless you can *definitely* trust them. Just because a hyperlink in an email message says it will direct you to your bank, it doesn't mean that is where you are being taken

- *always* make sure that computer security software (see Topic 1.32) is kept up to date and switched on

- never leave your computer unattended whilst you are logged on. Anyone can then use it to gain access to your files and other parts of the system. One solution is to 'lock' your screen so that it can only be unlocked by entering your password

- when shopping on the internet, always make sure that the website you are using to enter your payment details is *encrypted* (see Topic 1.32).

Tasks

1. Write down a definition of each of the following terms:
   a hacker
   b virus
   c malware.

2. Explain the difference between spyware and adware.

3. Explain why you should never reply to junk emails or open the files attached to them.

4. Produce an information leaflet which is to be given to new employees of a business whose computers are connected to the internet. The leaflet should explain some of the threats to the security of the business's data as well as their own personal data. Include some recommendations for how the users can reduce the risk of these problems occurring.

Topic 1.31

Data security (2)

Aims

By the end of this topic you should be able to:
- describe the main measures available to protect computer systems
- evaluate the usefulness of protection measures in a given scenario.

There are a number of different measures which can be taken to improve the security of a computer system. Some of the more common ones are covered in this topic.

Usernames and passwords

The commonest way to restrict access to a computer system is to give each user a username and password. The username helps to define the user for the network (for example by giving them access to the files they have saved, but not anyone else's) and is usually fixed by the person in charge of the system, either called the *system administrator* or the *network manager*. The username is often the way that different levels of *access rights* are managed (see below).

Many organisations use a common system for working out the username, for example in a business it might be based on the user's surname and the date they joined the organisation. This means that the network manager can identify who a user is by their username. Unfortunately it also means that anyone in the organisation can work out another person's username. This means that an extra layer of protection is needed: a password.

A password is a sequence of characters (text, numbers and other *characters* on the keyboard such as # or %) that the user needs to type into the computer after their username in order to gain access to the network. Users are usually able to change their password regularly: this helps to keep it a secret.

It is vital that the password is kept secret. Somebody who knows another person's username and password can use them to log onto the computer, change the password and then prevent the user from gaining access to their own files. There are some basic principles of how to keep a password secure:

- always use a password that is hard to guess. Your favourite football team or colour will be known by many people so should not be used
- a *strong password* will be a random collection of characters that should be difficult to guess; for example gs3T*a1@cgHU will be a better password than a *weak* password such as *chelsea*
- ideally, a different password should be used for every computer system you use: this should mean, for example, a different one for work and for an internet bank and a different one again for a home computer
- never write your password down: this could easily be seen by someone else
- change your password at frequent intervals.

Access rights

Individual users of a computer system are likely to only have access to parts of the system. For example, a worker in the sales department will be able to view product databases but will not be able to view records kept by the *personnel department* on how much each employee is paid. The person who will have the greatest access will be the *network manager*. This person will need to have access to the software which controls how the network is operated: this will include the *operating system* and the *network management system*. These systems allow the network manager to create new user accounts and define access rights for all the network users.

Physical restrictions

Usernames, passwords and access rights help to prevent unauthorised users gaining access to the network. Another way this can be achieved is by physical security measures. These are designed to prevent unauthorised users laying their hands on the computer system's hardware. Examples of physical restrictions include:

- in a shop or library, locating computers away from the main areas where members of the public might be found. If this isn't possible, then only very specific areas of the network will be available from these machines

- limiting the number of computers on the ground floor of an office building, to make it harder for thieves to steal them

- putting important computers such as network servers in a secure part of the building. This might be on the top floor or in a basement which can be sealed to prevent flooding

- ensuring that doors and windows are securely locked when computer rooms are not in use and protected by alarm systems.

Tasks

1 Explain the difference between a username and password.

2 David Shreeve uses the same password for every one of his sixteen different computer user accounts. The password is 'mayfavouriteteamischelsea'. David has written this password down in the first page of his diary. Explain to David what is wrong with his approach to using passwords and recommend ways in which he can increase the security of his data.

3 In Topic 1.30 you produced an information leaflet. Extend this leaflet to include advice on how to manage passwords.

Topic 1.32
Data security (3)

> **Aims**
>
> By the end of this topic you should be able to:
> - describe the main measures available to protect computer systems
> - evaluate the usefulness of protection measures in a given scenario.

Anti-malware software

The main type of anti-malware protection is provided by anti-virus software. Nowadays anti-virus protection comes as part of a suite of computer protection software together with anti-spam, anti-spyware and firewall protection.

Anti-virus software works in two ways:

- all files that are opened by a user or downloaded from a remote source, such as the internet or a memory stick, are scanned to see if they match samples of known virus programs that are stored in the anti-virus program's library. Any files that contain viruses are either blocked, deleted or have the virus element of them removed. For this reason it is important to keep anti-virus software up to date so that its library contains details of all known viruses

- any unusual activity on the computer is monitored by the anti-virus software. An example might be an attempt by a program to perform an unusual act such as downloading a file from the internet. If the activity matches anything the anti-virus software knows to be caused by a virus it will prevent the action from taking place.

Anti-spyware software works in a similar way – details of spyware programs are stored in a library and this is used to check all incoming files to see if they contain spyware. If they do the file is blocked.

Anti-spam software works by storing details of known SPAM addresses – when an incoming email message is sent from one of these addresses the message is diverted into a spam folder where it will be deleted after a few days.

Firewalls

A firewall is designed to prevent unauthorised access to a computer or network from other computers attached to it or connected over the internet. The basic way a firewall works is as follows:

- the firewall monitors all incoming and outgoing traffic to and from the computer or network

- any incoming or outgoing data that has not been requested by the computer is blocked. For example, if John selects a web page, his firewall will allow the request because the request came from a user on his computer. However, if a user connected to that web page then tries to gain access to John's computer, John's firewall will block the attempt as it wasn't requested by John or his computer.

Encryption

Encryption is used to protect data whilst it is being transferred between two computers over a network such as the internet. Data being transferred over the internet can easily be intercepted by unauthorised computers. One reason for this is that the system often uses telephone technology to transmit the data, and this can be hacked into. Data encryption works in the following way:

- data to be transmitted by computer A to computer B is first scrambled into a secret code by computer A's encryption software, using an *encryption key*
- the scrambled data is then transmitted over the internet to computer B
- computer B receives the scrambled data and then unscrambles it using the same encryption key used by computer A.

The same encryption principle can also be used to protect the data stored on a computer. The computer stores the data in encrypted form and the user is required to enter a password before the computer *decrypts* the data for them to use. In this way the data on portable and handheld devices such as laptops and PDA/smartphones can be protected – unless a thief knows the encryption password they will be unable to use the data stored on the device.

A very common use of data encryption is for making payments for goods and services on the internet. The customer's personal and payment information, such as address and credit card number, are typed into a form held on a *secure website*. The data is then encrypted before transmission over the internet. The address of secure websites always begin with the letters *https://* and a *padlock* symbol is displayed in the *status bar* at the bottom of the browser window displaying the page.

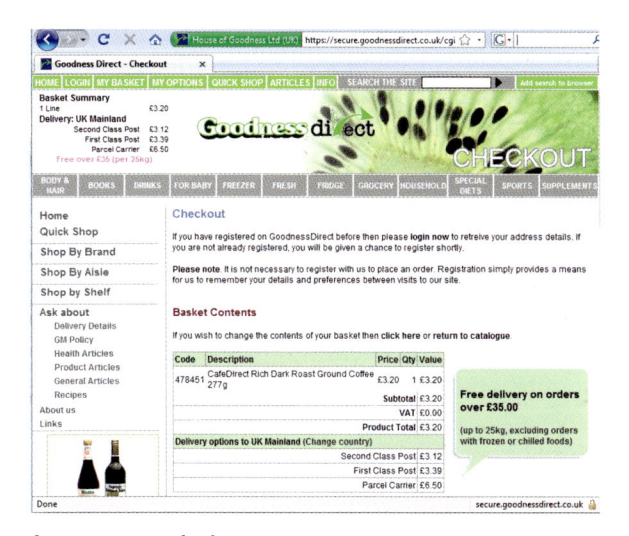

A secure website

Tasks

1. Describe how anti-virus software works.
2. Explain why it is important that anti-virus and anti-spyware software is kept up to date.
3. Explain in your own words how a firewall works.
4. Describe in your own words how data can be sent securely from one computer to another using data encryption.
5. Visit the websites of at least two banks and find out what security advice they offer to their customers about how they can help to prevent unauthorised use of their online bank account. Use the knowledge you gain from this to produce a leaflet aimed at all bank customers called 'How to protect your internet bank account'.

Topic 1.33

Systems to support e-commerce (1)

Aims

By the end of this topic you should be able to:

- **describe the systems needed to create, distribute, view and interact with web pages**
- **analyse the benefits and drawbacks to business organisations and customers of e-commerce**
- **assess the impact of e-commerce on business organisations and their customers.**

Many business organisations have a presence on the internet. Indeed some businesses, such as Amazon, do not have any traditional shops, doing all of their business through their web-stores. Many small business organisations have a website, and this is very important as a number of surveys have suggested that customers prefer to do business with an organisation which has one. The term e-commerce is used to refer to any business presence on the internet which helps the business to operate.

In this topic we will look at the systems needed by both the business and its customers so that they can use the internet for e-commerce.

A computer system needed by a customer to connect to the internet would typically include the following items:

- Computer system with web browser and email software:
  – a web browser is special software which is used to convert the *html code* – the language used to write and exchange websites – into a visual image displayed on the monitor
  – email software, sometimes included as part of diary management software (see Section 3), enables the user to send, receive and store email messages.
- A modem: this is a device which sends and receives data over the internet.
- An internet connection – in the UK at the time of writing this was mainly done over a telephone-based network called *ADSL* – this delivers *broadband* internet speeds of up to 8 megabytes per second. An older technology was to send data across the telephone at speeds of up to 56 kbps – over 100 times slower!
- An internet service provider: this is the organisation which provides you with an internet service and usually email facilities as well.
- Security software such as a firewall and anti-virus software.

Computer systems needed by a business wishing to do business on the internet:

- A *domain name* e.g. amazon.com or morrisons.co.uk which users can use to visit your website.
- A web server that hosts the organisation's website and sends it to users connected to the internet. This is either managed by the business itself or the organisation can pay to use a web-hosting service provided by another business. Whichever method is used it is important to have enough capacity to cope with all the users who visit the website at the same time.
- A website with secure shopping and payment facilities (sometimes provided by another organisation such as *Paypal*).

- A secure connection between the website and the organisation's order management, stock management, customer and finance databases.
- Security software to protect the organisation's systems from malicious attack.

Benefits and drawbacks of e-commerce for a customer

Benefits:
- shopping can be done from home. This saves the time and expense involved with visiting a shop
- shopping can be done at any time of the day
- home delivery
- a wider choice is available
- cheaper prices. Sometimes prices offered by internet suppliers are cheaper than in high street stores. *Price comparison* websites such as Kelkoo or PriceRunner can help by listing the prices charged by different online retailers for the same product.

Drawbacks:
- the customer may have to pay a delivery charge
- the customer may have to wait in for the delivery
- the customer needs to be able to trust the retailer to deliver the products as promised. This is easier if the business is well-known, but harder if they are a new or unknown business
- the customer needs to make sure that their payment details will be kept safely by the retailer
- sometimes retailers do not state the delivery time until after the products have been ordered. This might result in a delay of days or even weeks before the product is delivered.

Tasks

1. State two items of hardware a customer needs in order to be able to connect to the internet.
2. State one item of software a customer needs in order to be able to connect to the internet.
3. What are the following?
    - ISP
    - Domain name
    - Web-hosting service
4. Identify two benefits and two drawbacks to a customer of ordering their shopping from a supermarket's website.
5. Analyse the benefits and drawbacks to a customer of doing their shopping over the internet.

Topic 1.34

Systems to support e-commerce (2)

Aims

By the end of this topic you should be able to:
- describe the systems needed to create, distribute, view and interact with web pages
- analyse the benefits and drawbacks to business organisations and customers of e-commerce
- assess the impact of e-commerce on business organisations and their customers.

Benefits and drawbacks of e-commerce for a business

Benefits:

- The business can reach customers from all over the world, so potentially increasing the amount of sales income received.
- It is easier and cheaper to update the details on a website than it is to re-print a new version of a price list or catalogue.
- The business will need fewer sales staff as the website will handle most orders automatically. The business may also decide to operate fewer shops.
- The business can use the website to collect information from customers. For example the website could contain feedback forms where visitors can state what they think of the website. The website can also record how many visits it has received, when they have taken place and even the approximate location of computer used to make the visit.

Drawbacks:

- The business needs to make sure the website and the payment systems it uses are secure from attack by unauthorised users.
- The business needs to make sure that the website is kept up to date.
- The business needs to make sure it has the capacity to cope with the number of visits to the website as well as the amount of orders it generates.

Payment systems

There are a number of different ways that businesses can manage the taking of payments for orders made on their websites. The choice of system will depend on the following factors:

- whether the business wishes to host its own payment system or use the services of another business
- the cost of the payment system (hardware as well as security systems) and whether the business can afford them
- the size of the business: larger organisations tend to own and manage their own payment systems, smaller businesses tend to use other methods.

The main methods used are as follows:

- The business owns all the servers and security systems needed to operate its website as well as an online ordering and payment system. An example of a business which uses this method is Amazon.

Systems to support e-commerce (2)

Amazon's secure ordering page

- A business hosts its own website but pays another organisation to use its ordering and payment systems. An example of a business operating in early 2009 which provides this service to other organisations is PayPal.

PayPal

- A business hosts its own website but customers have to contact the firm directly (by email, telephone or post) to order and/or pay for products.

Tasks

1. In East Yorkshire a group of farmers and other food producers have created a website called www.theinternetfarmshop.com. Visit the website and look at the web page of each producer. What methods do they use to enable customers to order from them? Why do you think they use these methods?

2. Terry Palin owns a small butchers shop in York. Terry is well-known locally for the quality of his sausages and pies and is thinking of setting up a website where he can sell his products.
    a. What are the benefits and drawbacks to Terry of selling his products over the internet?
    b. Carry out some research on the internet into the types of websites and ordering systems used by similar retailers. What are the benefits and drawbacks of the systems used?
    c. Recommend a system which Terry could use to sell the products he displays on his website.

3. An uncle of yours tells you that he will never order anything from a website because he does not believe that online shopping is safe. Explain to him in your own words the actions that retailers take to reduce the risks involved in e-commerce.

Topic 1.35

Preparing for the examination

Aims

By the end of this topic you should be able to:
- understand how this unit will be assessed
- answer examination-type questions.

Unit A265 is assessed through a 1½ hour written examination paper. The paper will contain a number of questions based on a particular business or context.

Different questions will ask you to do different things. Basically, there are four things that are being tested on this paper:

1 Your knowledge of businesses and their communication systems.
For example, you might be asked to 'State two laws which businesses must follow.' All that is required in the answer is a list of two laws. You do not need to explain anything about the laws. These questions typically carry just 1 or 2 marks (1 for each item of knowledge you are asked to give).

2 Your ability to apply your knowledge to a problem or issue.
For example, you might be asked to describe two benefits to a customer of shopping online. In this question you would not get any marks for describing the benefits to the business.

3 Your ability to analyse issues.
Analysis means trying to understand an issue by using your existing knowledge or by looking at it from different perspectives. For example, you might be asked to 'Explain the impact on a business of complying with health and safety legislation.' Some of the impact might be beneficial, e.g. fewer accidents, but there will also be drawbacks, e.g. increased costs.

4 Evaluate issues and draw conclusions.
To evaluate means to assess or weigh up a situation. This can be done by considering the benefits and drawbacks and then coming to a conclusion. For example the question 'Assess the benefits and drawbacks of a business giving memory sticks to all its employees' is asking you to decide whether this is a good idea or not. You need to consider the benefits to the business of doing this, then the drawbacks, before finally recommending whether the business should do it or not.

Examination questions

1. Anne spends many hours at a computer and as a result might develop health problems. State one such possible health problem and describe how it might be solved. **(2 marks)**
(OCR, May 2007)

2. Jenny Jones is given a username and password so that she can use the head office computer network. Give one reason why Jenny should change her password frequently. **(1 mark)**
(OCR, May 2007)

Preparing for the examination   85

3   Discs R Us is planning to set up a website where customers can buy its products online.
    a Name one type of hardware that customers would need to use in order to view the website.
                                                                                    (1 mark)
    b Name one type of software that customers would need to use in order to access the website.
                                                                                    (1 mark)
    c State two benefits to Discs R Us of selling its products on a website.   (2 marks)
    d Describe two benefits to customers of shopping online.   (2 marks)
                                                                            (OCR, May 2007)

4   The head office network has a firewall installed. Describe how a firewall can restrict access to a head office network.   (2 marks)
                                                                            (OCR, May 2007)

5   A customer in the head office reception area is demanding to see all of her personal data held by Discs R Us. Under what circumstances is the customer entitled to see this data?
                                                                                    (2 marks)
                                                                            (OCR, May 2007)

6   Explain how the Computer Misuse Act helps to restrict unauthorised access to computer data.
                                                                                    (2 marks)
                                                                            (OCR, May 2008)

7   Consultants who work from home and visit customers' houses are provided with a laptop computer and a mobile phone by Colourful Homes Limited. Identify and explain two benefits to Colourful Homes Limited of giving mobile phones to its consultants.   (4 marks)
                                                                            (OCR, May 2008)

8   Colourful Homes Limited keeps only electronic copies of letters it sends to customers and suppliers. Analyse the advantages and disadvantages to Colourful Homes Limited of keeping only electronic copies of letters sent to customers and suppliers.   (6 marks)
                                                                            (OCR, May 2008)

9   A letter has been posted to customers containing incorrect information about an existing service. Assess the problems which this failure in service might cause for Colourful Homes Limited.   (6 marks)
                                                                            (OCR, May 2008)

10 State two ways in which a Public Limited Company is different to a Sole Trader. (2 marks)

11 A small fruit and vegetable shop is concerned that a new supermarket is taking away its customers. The shop is considering taking the following actions to remain competitive:
    i   cutting its prices by 20%
    ii advertising in the local newspaper
    iii introducing a home delivery service.

    Assess these actions, recommending which, if any, the business should take. Give reasons for your recommendations.   (6 marks)

12 Explain how a business could use market research to monitor how competitive it is.
                                                                                    (4 marks)

13 A new business is considering how it can provide effective after-sales service to customers. Identify and explain two ways in which after-sales service can be provided.   (4 marks)

14 A take-away restaurant is due to open near to a quiet residential area.
Identify and explain two actions the business can take to operate in a socially responsible way.
(4 marks)

15 A new business is considering whether it should back up its computer data.
a Explain two benefits to the organisation of backing up its computer data. (4 marks)
b Describe two features of an effective back-up system. (4 marks)

UNIT 2

DEVELOPING BUSINESS COMMUNICATION SYSTEMS

Unit 2: Developing business communication systems

Topic 2.1

❯ Business communication systems

Aims

By the end of this topic you should be able to:
- **describe the main elements of common business communication systems.**

In Unit 1 we looked at the main components of business and communication systems. We also looked at the business context in which these systems operate. In this unit we will explore in detail how businesses communicate and the systems they use. We will consider the impact that these systems have on the business as well as on people and other organisations. We will explore the strengths and weaknesses of these systems and learn how to make recommendations for improvements to them.

The following diagram summarises the main components of any business communication system:

- What message needs to be delivered?
- What system should be used to create and send the message? Hardware? Software? Storage?
- What method should be used to transmit the message?

The main components of a business communication system

The systems you will explore are those found in any small or medium-sized business organisation. They include systems based on standard office hardware and software (such as word processors, spreadsheets, databases and diary management software – these will be looked at in more detail in Unit 3). We will not look at the technicalities of how these systems work. Instead you will develop a broad understanding of what they consist of and how they operate. This will enable you to select systems and methods which are appropriate for particular situations. You will then also be able to make recommendations for improvements to both the systems and the communications they are used to create.

Case study

ICT systems in a school office.

A school office might contain the following systems:
- A computer network which enables office staff to view information about pupils and their parents. The system also has internet access to enable office staff to send and receive emails.
- A telephone system which enables staff to contact parents, teachers and others.
- A tannoy system to send voice messages to a speaker in each classroom.

A typical school office

Case study

ICT systems in a travel agency.

A travel agency might contain the following systems in each of its branches:
- A computer network that connects to the internet, enabling the travel agency to book flights, hotels and holiday packages on behalf of customers. The computers will also connect to the head office network in order to upload customer information to the organisation's central database.
- Telephones to contact customers as well as hotels and airlines.

A travel agency

Topic 2.2
Business communication methods

Aims

By the end of this topic you should be able to:
- describe the main purposes of business communication
- describe the main methods of business communication.

How many times have you communicated with someone today? The chances are you might have sent a text message, listened to a teacher, talked with a friend on a mobile phone or spoken face-to-face with a family member. Communication happens all the time both inside and outside businesses.

Communication can be defined as anything that enables a person or organisation to exchange information or ideas with another person or organisation.

In order for communication to take place the following things need to happen:

- A message is constructed – what the person or organisation wants to say.
- A method is decided upon to deliver the message – the method might be verbal (sound) or it might be visual (words or images).
- The sender transmits the message using a suitable medium (a verbal message might be delivered in person or using a telephone).
- The recipient receives the message and perhaps then replies with a message of their own.

Communication can be either one-way or two-way

One-way communication occurs when the sender (transmitter) of the message does not know if it has been received or understood by anyone. For example, a radio broadcast is an example of one-way communication. The radio broadcaster does not receive any *feedback* from the listeners so the broadcaster does not know if their message has

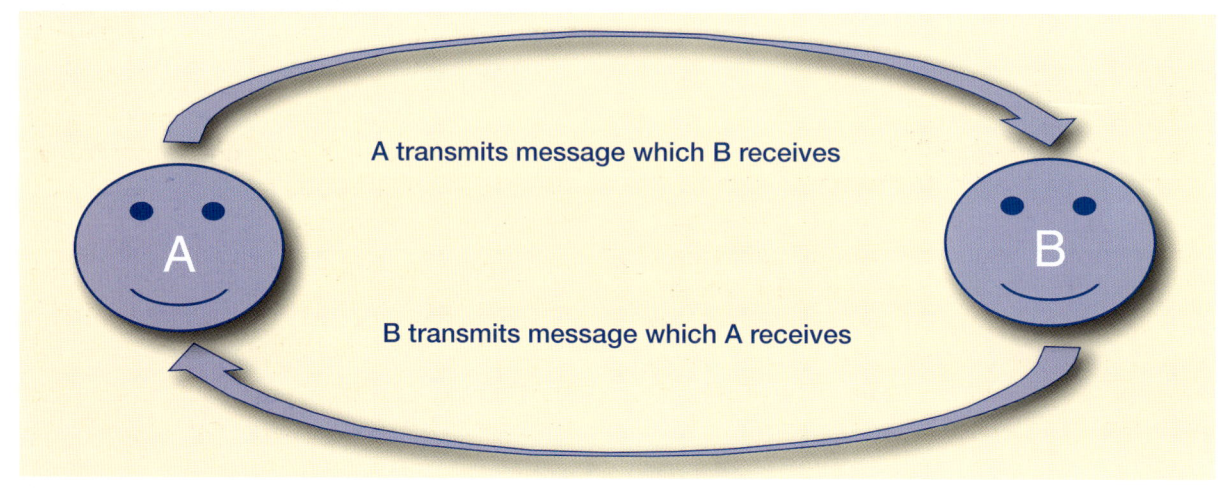

A transmits message which B receives

B transmits message which A receives

One-way and two-way communication

been understood or even received at all. Examples of one-way communication include leaflets, websites, adverts and television programmes.

Two-way communication occurs when the sender is able to receive feedback from the receiver which helps them to understand whether their message has been received and understood. Two-way communication includes face-to-face discussions, telephone calls, letters and emails. Sometimes, as in a telephone conversation, the feedback is instant; with other situations, such as emails or letters, the feedback may take some time to receive.

There are a number of different communication methods available to business organisations. These include:

- Verbal communication
  Examples include meetings, telephone conversations, radio adverts or podcasts.
- Written communication
  Examples include leaflets, letters, emails, text messages, brochures.
- Visual communication
  Examples include diagrams, photographs, television adverts.
- Multimedia communication
  This includes any product which combines verbal, written and visual methods. Examples include websites, presentations and some advertisements.

Internal communication

This is any communication which takes place inside the business, for example from one employee to another or one part of the organisation to another. As we will see in a later topic, memoranda are normally an example of internal communication because they are sent from one part of the business to another.

External communication

This is any communication between the business and organisations and individuals outside it. An example would be a letter sent by the business to a customer, or even a letter sent to the home address of an employee.

Private communication

Private communications are not designed to be received by anyone other than the intended recipient. For example, a business planning to develop a new product would not want news of this development to be given to its competitors.

Public communication

This is any message where the business does not restrict who receives it. Public messages should not contain any information the organisation wishes to keep secret.

Factors affecting the choice of method for a particular message

There are a number of things to take into account when choosing a communication method. These include the following:

- How complicated is the message? Straightforward messages may only need to be heard once; a more complex message, or one that contains a lot of information, may need to be written down so the receiver can study it more carefully.
- Does a permanent copy of the message need to be kept? For example, does the receiver need to be able to refer to the information contained in the message at a later date?
- Does the sender require feedback that the message has been received and understood? If so a verbal method might be needed.
- How many people need to receive the message? The larger the number of receivers,

the more likely it is that the message will be broadcast, for example on a website, a radio programme or via a *mailshot letter*.

- Is the message confidential or can anyone receive it?

- How quickly does the message need to be delivered? Verbal methods are generally the quickest method, but it might take time to contact the person by telephone.

Tasks

1 Draw a diagram to illustrate the difference between one-way and two-way communication.

2 A salesperson needs to deliver a message to a customer. Describe the stages which the salesperson will go through in order to transmit their message and make sure it is understood.

3 What is meant by *multimedia* communication?

4 Explain the difference between the following terms:

   a internal and external communication

   b public and private communication.

5 You have been asked to deliver a secret message to fifty people who all work for the same organisation at the same location. How will you deliver this message? Describe the factors you took into account in order to choose this method.

Topic 2.3

Internal business communication (1)

Aims

By the end of this topic you should be able to:
- **describe the features of the media that are used by business organisations to communicate information**
- **assess the benefits and drawbacks of the media for business communications**
- **select and justify appropriate methods and media for business communications.**

A lot of the communication carried out by a business takes place inside the organisation between its employees. Examples include:

- a product development team informing sales staff about a new product
- a telephone operator taking a telephone message which they pass on to a colleague
- all staff being informed of a major development in the organisation such as a reorganisation of the working day
- the network manager reminding staff to keep their passwords secret.

Staff transmitting these messages should use the most appropriate method to deliver the message. In the previous topic you learned some of the factors to take into account when choosing a transmission method. In this topic we will look at the different written media available. You will learn how to create these documents in Unit 3.

Internal written communication

Memorandum

A memorandum (usually shortened to *memo*) is a printed document which is sent from one employee to others. A memo is usually sent from a *manager* or *supervisor* to members of their team and provides information or details of a new policy. The use of memos is declining and has largely been replaced by email.

Newsletter

Many large organisations, often with branches in different places, use newsletters to help keep their many employees informed about current events in the business. Newsletters can be quite expensive to produce and print. For this reason many organisations have now replaced a printed newsletter with an electronic one which is either emailed to staff or put on the company *intranet*.

Business report

A business report is a formal document which summarises the results of research which has been carried out and provides recommendations for action. Business reports usually include the following sections:

- Introduction – including the name of the report, who produced it and when.
- Terms of reference – why the report has been produced, who requested it and what they wanted the report to cover.
- Evidence – the results of the research obtained.
- Recommendations – the action which should be taken by the business in response to the investigation carried out.
- Conclusion – a summary of the report and its findings.

Business reports are often highly *confidential* – meaning they are designed for just a few members of staff to study, in order to help them take important decisions. For example, the directors of a business might ask for a report to be written to help them decide which of two offices to close down.

Email

Email is rapidly becoming one of the main internal communication methods. Most organisations using email over a network provide staff with an electronic address book containing the email addresses of all staff. A user can then select the option to send a message to all staff in the address book. They can also edit the address book to create lists of groups of staff, for example everyone in the finance department.

A drawback of using email is that recipients need to have access to their email account in order to view their messages. This may be difficult for staff employed in a factory, or those who spend a lot of time travelling. Another problem is that if a user has access to their own private email address at work they can forward copies of messages out of the organisation.

Notice board

Sometimes an employee might choose to pin a document on a notice board. Anyone who walks past the notice board can then view the message. Benefits of using a notice board to display messages include: fewer documents are printed and people can read the message several times. Drawbacks of using a notice board include: not everyone will see the document, especially if another message gets pinned over the top of it; documents may become damaged, torn or accidentally removed; and a notice board is not suitable for confidential information as it is not possible to control who reads it.

Intranet

An intranet works like an electronic version of a notice board but on a much larger scale. An intranet is a website which can only be viewed by people inside the organisation. Usually this is because the web pages are not 'published' on the internet but are hosted on the organisation's own private network.

The intranet will contain information for employees, as well as documents which they can download to their computer. These might include an electronic version of the organisation's newsletter as well as forms (e.g. an expenses claim form).

Sometimes the pages are published on the internet to enable specific people from outside the organisation to view them (this might include suppliers or consultants who work for the organisation on a temporary basis from home). This is called an extranet. In this case authorised users are given a username and password in order to log onto the extranet.

Tasks

1 Why are memos being replaced by email as an internal communication method?

2 State two drawbacks of using email to send important messages to staff.

3 You have decided to use a notice board to pin an important message to all staff who work in a hospital. Describe the benefits and drawbacks of using this method.

4 Explain the difference between an intranet and an extranet.

5 Your school has decided that all messages and information for staff will be published on an intranet. Discuss the benefits and drawbacks of this method. Overall, do you think this is a good idea? Give reasons for your answers.

Topic 2.4

Internal business communication (2)

Aims

By the end of this topic you should be able to:
- **describe the features of the media used by business organisations to communicate information**
- **assess the benefits and drawbacks of the media for business communications**
- **select and justify appropriate methods and media for business communications.**

As well as written media such as memos and emails, much internal communication is done using verbal methods. In this topic we will look at the main ones used.

Internal verbal communication

Meetings

A meeting takes place when two or more people get together to discuss ideas or exchange information. For example, a team of customer service workers might hold a weekly meeting where they discuss issues affecting their work and receive information from their manager. Meetings can be either formal or informal.

A formal business meeting

A formal meeting will be planned in advance. Participants will be sent a Notice of Meeting inviting them to attend and an Agenda which lists the topics to be discussed. A record of what was discussed and decided at each meeting (called the minutes) will be written down and given to all participants after each meeting.

An informal meeting is often not planned, will not have any documentation produced and may be used to hold a short discussion about a topic.

Sometimes meetings are also held which involve large numbers of staff. For example all the nurses in a hospital might hold a monthly meeting where they can learn about new medical techniques or hospital rules. These meetings might involve discussions, briefings and presentations.

- A discussion involves an exchange of ideas and opinions and is usually held to try to find out what people think of an idea, or to persuade them to agree to a proposal.
- A briefing is a one-way transmission of information with little opportunity for discussion. The purpose is to provide information.
- A presentation is a talk (often accompanied by *visual aids* such as an electronic slideshow) designed to provide information on a complex or detailed topic. The presentation might be part of a briefing or be designed to spark a discussion afterwards.

For example, a headteacher might wish to make changes to timings of the school day. S/he might hold a meeting with all staff to discuss the proposal and hear the views of teachers and other staff. The meeting might begin with a slideshow presentation where they present their plans for the new school day. Some time later, once the new school day timings have been decided, the headteacher might organise another meeting of all staff, this time to brief them about the changes that have been decided.

Meetings where a group of people meet together are called *face-to-face* meetings. Non face-to-face meetings include telephone conferencing and video conferencing (discussed below).

Telephone

Telephones can be used to communicate information between staff. This is especially useful if the other member of staff is at a different location such as another branch or at a meeting with customers (in which case they can be contacted on their mobile telephone).

Telephone conferencing is a facility that enables a group of people to take part in the same conversation from their own individual telephones. A benefit of this technology is that it can be cheaper and take up less time than organising a face-to-face meeting where people have to travel. This could save the organisation thousands of pounds in travel and hotel expenses. A drawback of using this method is that participants cannot see each other, so it is hard to hold a discussion as each participant cannot see when someone else is ready to speak.

Video conferencing

This works in a very similar way to telephone conferencing. The main difference is that video technology is used to capture moving images of each participant as well as their voice. This is discussed in more detail in Topic 2.8.

The choice of an appropriate method to deliver a verbal message will depend on a number of factors. These include:

- the ease and cost of organising a face-to-face meeting, especially when participants might be working in different countries
- how many people are required to attend. Are your school assemblies delivered as a briefing or are they an opportunity for whole-school discussion?
- the need for discussion. A briefing, for example, might be better delivered in an emailed document or by being placed on an intranet.

Tasks

1. Name two documents produced before a formal business meeting.
2. Name the document produced during a formal business meeting and explain why it is produced.
3. You need to discuss an important issue with four other colleagues. You all work in the same office. Which method will you use? Explain why.
4. You need to discuss an important issue with four other colleagues. You each work in different countries. Which method will you use? Explain why.
5. Explain the benefits and drawbacks of holding a discussion with eight other people using telephone conferencing.

Topic 2.5

External business communication (1)

Aims

By the end of this topic you should be able to:
- describe the features of the media used by business organisations to communicate information
- assess the benefits and drawbacks of the media for business communications
- select and justify appropriate methods and media for business communications.

Businesses need to communicate with other organisations, as well as individuals such as customers. Just as with internal methods, a variety of formal/informal written/verbal methods are used.

External written communication

Individual letters

A letter is a formal document sent by an organisation to another organisation or individual. The letter may contain information or answers to questions raised previously, perhaps in a letter sent to the business. You will learn how to create a business letter later in this unit.

The main benefits of sending a letter include: if the business keeps a copy it will have a record of what the letter contains; the receiver will also be able to keep the letter and refer to it on later occasions. A drawback with letters is the time it takes to deliver – usually between one and three days, as well as the costs of printing the letter and paying a postal charge.

Personalised mailshots

Another type of letter is a personalised mailshot. A mailshot is a letter which is designed to be sent to a large number of people. An example would be a letter sent by a car retailer to all its previous customers, informing them of some new cars for sale. Mailshot letters are sent using mail-merge (you will learn how to create a mail-merged letter in Unit 3). A benefit for the business of using mail-merge to create letters is that it is relatively straightforward. A drawback for customers is that it makes it easier for businesses to send *junk mail* – publicity material that the receiver usually throws away.

Flyers/leaflets/brochures

These are documents designed to provide information to potential customers about the products for sale by the business. A flyer is a single sheet of paper, usually printed on only one side, containing an advertisement for a business or event. Flyers are often distributed inside newspapers or magazines. They are often produced by local organisations or small businesses. A leaflet is a more complex document than a flyer. For example, it might consist of a sheet of A4 paper folded in half and printed on both sides to create a four-page leaflet. A leaflet will contain more information than a flyer and will probably be of higher quality, often being professionally printed and in colour. A brochure will contain several pages, often stapled together, and will include more information than a leaflet. A brochure might provide details of all the products a manufacturer produces.

Internet and email

Many organisations have a website to communicate information to other people. The main purpose of the website will vary according to the needs of each organisation but is likely to include some or all of the following:

- to give customers and others basic information about the organisation
- to provide information about the organisation's activities or products
- to sell the business's products or services
- to enable customers and others to download information such as product guides or where to buy the organisation's products.

Email is becoming an increasingly common way for organisations to communicate with customers and others. Some businesses encourage email communication by providing a feedback form on their website. People who wish to contact the organisation can complete the form and send the information by clicking a *submit* button. If they have provided an email address the business will be able to reply by email.

Another way to collect email addresses from customers, for example, is to request the address when a product is ordered and ask the customer if they wish to receive email messages from the business (to meet the terms of the Data Protection Act). If they agree, then the business will add them to an email list. The messages sent can be *multimedia* messages containing text, images and animations.

There are no hard and fast rules for how to communicate by email. Some people use very formal language and write emails as if they are a formal business letter. Other people send emails that are less formal and read like an informal conversation. The best rule to adopt if you are not sure how your recipient likes to communicate is to send a relatively formal message first.

Tasks

1 State two benefits and two drawbacks of sending information to a customer in a letter.

2 Explain the main differences between a flyer, a leaflet and a brochure.

3 Visit the websites of five different schools. What would you say is the *main* purpose of each website?

4 Collect all the publicity material included in a newspaper (for example a free local newspaper or a Sunday newspaper). Sort them into flyers, leaflets and brochures. What is the main purpose of each document? How effective are they in communicating their messages?

5 Visit the websites of the following organisations operating in your local area: a retailer; a public-sector organisation such as a school or hospital; a local sports club such as a Sunday league cricket team. What is the main purpose of each website? How effective are they in communicating their messages?

Topic 2.6

External business communication (2)

Aims

By the end of this topic you should be able to:
- describe the features of the media used by business organisations to communicate information
- assess the benefits and drawbacks of the media for business communications
- select and justify appropriate methods and media for business communications.

External verbal communication

The two main groups of people a business organisation will speak to are its customers and suppliers. In this topic we will cover how businesses talk with their customers.

Face-to-face meetings with customers

The two main types of face-to-face meetings with customers are:

- formal discussions between a salesperson and a potential business customer which takes place at the customer's place of work. These meetings are held to discuss the terms of a large order, perhaps costing several thousand pounds. Sometimes many meetings might be held to sort out issues such as price and delivery times

- informal discussions which take place in a shop between a salesperson and a potential customer. A typical exchange might occur in an electrical shop where a salesperson demonstrates how a product works, what its benefits are and attempts to persuade the customer to buy the product.

The main benefit of face-to-face meetings for the business is that they enable sales staff to get instant feedback from the potential customer about what they think about the product and whether they are likely to buy it. The salesperson might be able to deal with any objections the customer might have about the product and so persuade them to buy it. A drawback with face-to-face meetings is that they can be very time-consuming – a travelling salesperson might only be able to meet with two or three customers in a single day.

Telephone

Telephones are an important point of contact between the customer and the business. A business might speak with customers by telephone in the following situations:

- to provide the customer with information about a product
- to take a customer's order over the telephone
- to deal with a customer's complaint about a product or to help them solve problems with it
- to contact a customer to find out if they received good customer service from the business.

A benefit of using the telephone to speak with customers is that more customers can be dealt with. Telephone conversations are also cheaper to organise than face-to-face meetings. A drawback is that the two people cannot see each other, so cannot respond to the other person's *body language*.

Many business organisations now operate *call centres* where all customer calls are dealt with by a large team of telephone operators. Sometimes these call centres are located in foreign countries such as India where there are a large number of English speakers. A benefit for a business of operating a call centre is that they can be cheaper to run, particularly if they are located in a country where wages are lower than in the UK. A drawback is that customers sometimes find them impersonal.

There are a number of rules which business users of a telephone should follow. These include:

- always answer the phone promptly – never leave it ringing for more than five rings
- always give your name when receiving the call. Find out the name of the person you are speaking with and refer to them by their name
- when calling someone, always ask if it is convenient for them to speak to you. If not, ask when it would be convenient to phone again.

A number of organisations try to increase their sales by telephoning people at random and attempting to persuade them to buy their product or service. This is called *cold-calling*. Businesses use it because they find they can sell more this way than if they simply wait for customers to contact them. However, many customers do not like it, especially if they are a victim of *silent-calling*.

Silent-calling happens because many businesses use a computer to dial customer numbers. When the potential customer picks up their phone the call is only then transferred to a salesperson who can speak to the customer. If there aren't any salespeople free to take the call then the customer hears silence at the end of their phone. Many people do not like to receive silent calls and the organisations which make these calls can be fined by the UK telephone regulator OFCOM (Office of Communications).

Tasks

For each of the following situations, recommend a suitable communication method (or a combination of methods) to deliver the message. Also state whether each method is internal or external and verbal or written. For each method you recommend explain why you have chosen it.

1 A business wishes to advise all five thousand of its existing customers about an exciting new offer.

2 A business needs to contact a specific customer to inform them that a product they have returned to a shop for a repair is now ready for collection.

3 A manager wishes to hold a discussion with one of his/her employees about their recent job performance.

4 A customer wishes to find out the location of their nearest branch of a pet care shop.

5 The finance manager of a business wishes to contact all employees to let them know they will be paid a day early at the end of the month.

6 A human resource manager wishes to contact five job applicants to invite them for interview. The interview is in two weeks' time. The manager needs to know if each person will be attending the interview. The applicants also need information about when and where the interview will take place as well as travel directions and details of a task they will carry out during the interview.

Topic 2.7

Communication devices (1)

Aims

By the end of this topic you should be able to:
- describe the main features of communication devices
- evaluate the usefulness of communication devices in a given scenario.

In Unit 1 we looked at laptops and other computing devices used by business organisations. In this topic we will look at some of the main devices used by business organisations to enable them to carry out internal and external communication.

Facsimile machines (fax)

The fax machine is still a very important communication device. A fax machine consists of a scanner and a printer, connected to a telephone line. To send a fax of a document you first need to put the document into the fax machine. The machine will then scan the document to create a digital file containing all the data needed to be able to print a copy of the document. The machine then dials the telephone number of the phone that is connected to the recipient's fax machine. When they are connected together, the data file is sent over the telephone line to the receiving fax machine, where a copy of the original document is printed.

The benefits of sending documents by fax are: visual information such as charts and diagrams can be sent; sending a fax is quicker than sending the same document by post. The drawbacks are: it can be more expensive and fiddly to send the document by fax than sending it as an email attachment because you have to pay for the machine and the telephone call. Also, the contents of a fax can be read by anyone who is standing near the fax machine as it prints out the message. Fax is a good way of sending a copy of a paper document to another person, however a modern alternative would be to scan the document onto a computer and send the file as an email attachment.

Mobile phones

The mobile phone has become a very important business communication device over the past few years. Over time, the number of functions on a mobile phone has become greater in number and more complex. Originally, a mobile phone could just be used to hold a verbal conversation. Then texting was added. You learned in Topic 1.26 about Personal Digital Assistants; these days, many mobile phones also include PDA functions on their phone (known as smartphones). The business uses of a mobile phone now include: internet access, sending and receiving of emails, electronic diary management and even word processor, database and spreadsheet software use. Apart from the specific benefits of each of these functions (most of which are covered in Unit 3), the benefits and drawbacks to a business of giving its workers mobile phones include:

Benefits
- the business can contact its employees when they are away from the office
- employees can contact the business when they are away from the office
- employees can contact other employees when they are away from the office.

Drawbacks

- mobile phones are still generally more expensive to buy and operate compared with traditional *landline* telephones
- employees may feel under pressure to take calls from fellow employees at inconvenient times, e.g. when driving or whilst they are not supposed to be working.

Tasks

1 Draw a simple diagram to show how a document can be transmitted from one person to another by fax.

2 Describe the benefits and drawbacks of sending a document by fax.

3 You have been asked to send a copy of a 200 page document to a colleague in Australia. They need it by tomorrow. You do not have an electronic version of the document. Explain how you will send them a copy. Give reasons for your chosen method.

4 Choose a mobile telephone (perhaps the one that you use). Write a list of all its features. For each feature, state at least one *business* use.

5 A business has a number of employees who work from home and spend a lot of their time travelling and visiting clients. They have each been given a smartphone for business use.
  a Explain the benefits and drawbacks to the business of providing these smart phones to its home-based workers.
  b Explain the benefits and drawbacks to the workers of being given a smart phone by their employer.
  c Do you think that businesses should provide smartphones for their employees? Explain your answer.

Topic 2.8
Communication devices (2)

Aims

By the end of this topic you should be able to:
- **describe the main features of communication devices**
- **evaluate the usefulness of communication devices in a given scenario.**

Video conferencing

Video conferencing is a technology which enables two or more people to hold a face-to-face meeting without being in the same room. There are many different types of video conferencing systems but they all essentially consist of the same things:

- each location uses a video camera and microphone to capture a moving image and the sound of the participants at that location. This data is then transmitted to the other video conferencing locations, either using telephone or internet technology

- the sound and moving images from the other participants is displayed on a monitor or projection screen.

In this way each participant can both see and hear all the other participants in the meeting.

Video conferencing is typically used by businesses which have several branches in different countries and wish to hold regular short meetings with staff in these branches.

Benefits of video conferencing:

- It is better than a telephone conference because each participant can both see as well as hear all the other participants. This means they can see their body language and also know when someone wants to speak.

- People can hold face-to-face meetings without travelling to a single venue. This will save the costs of travel and hotel accommodation. The time spent not travelling can then be used to carry out other productive work.

Drawbacks of video conferencing:

- It is expensive. Even a relatively small video conferencing system can cost several thousand pounds. However, this may soon pay for itself in terms of reduced travel costs.

- Although better than voice-only telephone conferencing, the interactions between users will still not be as good as in a face-to-face meeting. This is sometimes because of a poor connection across the internet or telephone network.

Satellite navigation systems

This is another relatively new communications technology. One of the main business uses is for in-car navigation (sat nav). These systems work in the following way:

- the sat nav device contains software which includes a road map database and a system which calculates the best route to take between two locations

- the device also contains a transmitter/receiver which sends and receives signals from a satellite orbiting the earth. The signals are used to determine the exact location of the car on the map database

- the user enters their intended destination into the sat nav (e.g. the postcode)

- the sat nav device compares this with the present location and calculates the best route to take

- whilst the car is being driven, the sat nav device displays the current location of the car on a map on its display screen and gives the driver instructions as to which route to take to get to the destination.

Satellite navigation systems are of benefit to business drivers: these include sales representatives and delivery drivers. They do not have to plan their journey and the system estimates how long it will take to arrive. Many systems also receive data about road conditions, alerting drivers to accidents on their route for example. A drawback is that the map database can become very out of date. The routes may not always be suitable. There have been several stories of lorry drivers becoming stuck on narrow lanes which their sat nav has directed them down!

Radio-frequency identification (RFID) systems

RFID is a relatively new invention (an *emerging technology*) which is beginning to be used by businesses. An RFID system typically consists of the following parts:

- an RFID tag. This is a small radio transmitter attached to a product or device. The RFID tag stores and transmits data that is unique to the tag (and so also to the product to which it is attached). You can think of this data as being similar to a *barcode* – except that every tin of a particular brand of baked beans will have the same barcode – with RFID each individual tin will have its own unique radio signal

- an RFID transponder. This is a device which detects, receives and stores radio signals from an RFID tag

- a host computer. This receives data uploaded to it from the RFID transponder.

Some uses of RFID:

- a refrigerator could record when items have been removed from and returned to it. Items which are not returned could then be automatically ordered from a supermarket website

- items dispatched to customers from an online retailer could be automatically tracked. Transponders inside a fleet of delivery vehicles could be used to identify in which van a particular package has been put

- RFID tags can be implanted on (or even inside) animals, enabling the location of a pet dog to be monitored

- attendance registers in schools could be operated automatically if each pupil were given their own RFID tag.

Benefits of RFID: RFID enables the automatic tracking of objects which have a tag attached to them. This reduces the costs involved in manually recording the location of the object. It can also reduce the costs of monitoring and replacing stock in a warehouse (or even in the home) if the system were linked to an automatic re-ordering system.

Tasks

1. Describe in your own words how video conferencing works.
2. Explain two benefits and two drawbacks of video conferencing.
3. Explain in your own words how an in-car satellite navigation system works.
4. State two other possible uses of satellite navigation technology.
5. Explain one benefit and one drawback for businesses of using in-car satellite navigation.
6. Carry out research to identify and then describe three possible uses of RFID technology not mentioned above.

Topic 2.9
> Stakeholders

Aims

By the end of this topic you should be able to:
- identify the main types of stakeholder
- describe the main interests of selected stakeholders
- analyse how the interests of selected stakeholders may conflict with each other and the business organisation
- assess the impact of business activity on stakeholders.

In the previous topics in this unit we have looked at some of the communication systems, devices and technologies used by business organisations. In the rest of this unit we will be exploring how the impact of these systems can be assessed and ways in which new improved systems can be developed. In this topic we will look at some of the main groups of people who are affected by businesses and their communication systems. These people are called stakeholders.

Definition

A stakeholder is anyone who has an interest in the activities of a business organisation. Usually this is because they are in some way affected by them.

The main stakeholders

Owners (and directors)

The owners are the people who have invested their money into the business. They may also be the people who set up the business in the first place. They choose what to do with the profit earned by the business – for example, they can either re-invest it or keep it for themselves. The owners want the business to be successful – and this usually means making a large profit. The directors (the people who run the business on behalf of the owners) are interested in the same things – this is usually because their own pay is linked to the amount of profit the business makes.

Employees (including managers)

Employees are the people who work for the business. They include the managers who run the business in the way that the owners and directors want. Employees are interested in *job security* – they do not want to worry about possibly losing their job. They also want to earn a high income, and will want to work in a pleasant and safe environment.

Customers

Customers want to buy high-quality goods and services – and they want to pay as little as possible for them. If they are not satisfied that the products they buy offer good *value for money* then they may go to a competitor in future.

Suppliers

Suppliers provide the business with the things it needs in order to make its products and operate as an organisation. It wants to be paid as much as possible for the things it supplies, and it wants to be paid on time.

Communities

Many people's lives are indirectly affected by the actions of business organisations. These might include the family who struggle to sleep because of traffic leaving a factory late at night, or football fans whose favourite team can only survive because it is sponsored by a local business. If global warming is caused, in part, by the actions of oil producers and car manufacturers then everyone on the planet is affected by their actions.

Government

The government is interested in the success and failure of businesses for many different reasons. For example, governments receive part of their income from a tax on business profits – the more profits businesses make the more revenue the government receives. Also, governments are elected by voters, many of whom are employees, so governments pass laws which help to protect the interests of workers. However, the government knows that these laws help to increase business costs – this might be unpopular with business owners and also result in some businesses closing down. So there are limits on what governments force businesses to do.

Conflicts between stakeholders

Each stakeholder wants different things from the business and these do not always coincide. For example, one way a business can make large profits for its owners is by increasing its prices and cutting its costs. Increasing prices is bad news for customers, especially if they have little choice but to buy from a particular business. Cutting costs might be achieved by making some employees redundant, reducing the wages of those that remain and cutting the prices it pays to suppliers. The business might also decide to stop sponsoring a local sports club and cut the amount of money it spends on controlling pollution from its factory.

Impact of business activity on stakeholders

Some stakeholders will benefit from particular business actions whilst others will lose out. However, it is ultimately the owners and directors who have to decide what is best for the business (within the limits set by the laws passed by the government). Sometimes they might decide to earn as much profit as possible; other times they might decide to sacrifice some profits in order to keep other stakeholders happy.

Tasks

1 Name four stakeholders. Describe what their main interests are.

2 Who are the main stakeholders in a school? What are they interested in?

3 For each of the following news headlines, explain which stakeholders will gain and which ones will lose out.
   a 'Factory workers achieve 30% pay increase.'
   b 'Government raises business taxes to a record high level.'
   c 'Petrol station profits jump to new high.'
   d 'Amount spent on sponsorship by businesses falls to new low.'
   e 'New government health and safety laws will cost £800 million to implement.'

4 A car manufacturer announces that it is planning to build a new factory on land which is currently used as a country park by the residents of a small town. Which stakeholders are likely to be affected by this development? Explain how.

5 Mary Fischer is an unemployed single mother with two children. She lives opposite the entrance to a supermarket. The supermarket has announced it is extending its opening times to 24 hours a day and is advertising for people to work the night shift. Explain how Mary might be affected by this development.

Topic 2.10

The role of business communication systems in the success or failure of organisations

Aims

By the end of this topic you should be able to:

- assess the impact on business organisations of effective or ineffective communication systems.

In the previous topic we looked at the main *stakeholders* who are affected by the actions of business organisations. In this topic we will consider how they are affected by good and bad business communications.

What causes poor communication? Communication barriers

In Topic 2.2 we looked at how communication occurs when a message is transmitted from the sender to a receiver. The sender also has to decide what the best method to transmit the message is. Sometimes the message received may not be the one that the sender intended – this is the main way that *communication problems* can happen.

There are a number of reasons for poor communication between the sender and the receiver. These are sometimes called *barriers to communication*.

Attitudes

The mood of the people taking part in a discussion might cause problems. For example, two people might not get along with each other and so they find it difficult to hold a sensible discussion.

Language and cultural issues

A salesperson talking with a customer using a second language might mis-translate or misunderstand what the customer has said. The salesperson might also use technical terms which the customer doesn't understand.

Organisational issues

A business might be organised in a very *hierarchical way* (see Topic 1.3). As a result, messages sent by the directors might be misunderstood by managers and so the message received by the operatives may be incorrect. A business might have several branches, and communication between workers in different locations can be difficult.

Poor choice of medium

In 2003, employees of a business in Manchester were shocked to receive text messages from their employer telling them that they had been made redundant and would no longer receive any pay. Many of the workers felt it would have been more appropriate to receive the message in a face-to-face meeting with their managers.

Stakeholder impact of poor communication systems

Employees:

- Employees in a hierarchical organisation might feel very distant from the decision-makers at the top of the organisation. This might lower their morale as they do not feel their opinions matter to the owners and directors. This might result in them working less hard and so becoming less *productive*.

- Employees might make mistakes if they do not receive correct information from colleagues.

- Badly-designed computer systems which fail or work slowly can cause delays which can be frustrating and stressful.

Customers:

- Customers may choose to buy from a competitor if the messages they receive from the business are incorrect or confusing.

- Customers may choose to buy from a competitor if the business's website is poorly-designed or does not enable them to buy products online.

Suppliers:

- Suppliers may deliver the wrong product if they have not understood the customer's requirements exactly.

- The business might stop buying from the supplier if they cannot provide them with exactly what they want.

Tasks

1 Use the internet to visit a number of online retailers. Choose one website you find easy to use. Describe how this website helps the business to have a positive impact on its stakeholders.

2 Visit the website http://www.webpagesthatsuck.com/. Choose a business website you think is particularly poor. Explain how the business's stakeholders might be negatively affected by its website.

Topic 2.11

Capabilities and limitations of ICT-based systems

Aims

By the end of this topic you should be able to:
- describe factors affecting the effectiveness of ICT-based systems
- evaluate ICT-based systems from different perspectives.

In the previous topic we looked at some of the negative effects on stakeholders of poor business communication. In this topic we will look at some of the things that can affect the success or failure of an ICT-based business communication system.

Factors affecting the success or failure of a new ICT-based system

Costs (start-up and operating)

There are two main types of costs involved in setting up a new business communication system:

- Start-up costs are costs that are paid to design and develop the new system. Sometimes these can be very expensive; for example, a new computer system for the National Health Service in the UK is expected to cost over £20 billion (a billion is a thousand million!) to develop by the time it is fully operational. Development costs will include some or all of the following:
  - costs of researching and designing the new system
  - cost of buying or building all the hardware and software needed by the system
  - cost of testing the system and solving any problems
  - cost of training staff to use the system.
- Running costs are the day-to-day costs of making the system work. This will include some or all of the following:
  - wages of staff who operate, maintain and repair the system
  - cost of electricity
  - cost of replacement parts e.g. replacing broken keyboards or hard-drives
  - costs of training new staff to use the system.

Ease-of-use

A system that is easy to use will require less training for staff in how to use it. This will reduce the amount spent setting up and operating the system. A website that is easy to use will result in more people using it and increased sales.

Fitness for purpose

A system that is fit-for-purpose is one that will do everything that is expected of it. Common reasons why ICT systems are not fit-for-purpose include: systems that crash because the software is badly written; websites that fail to open because there are too many people trying to access them at the same time; and systems that do not have adequate security measures in place to protect personal data. All of these are reasons why users lose confidence in a system and, in the case of customers, do business elsewhere.

Security

A computer system should have in place enough security measures to keep the data secure. Systems which are insecure, or where customers think their data will not be safe, are unlikely to help a business become successful.

Health and safety

Systems should be safe for their operators to use. This includes the working patterns of the users. Health and safety issues were covered in Topic 1.12

Environmental sustainability

ICT systems should help the organisation to minimise its impact on the environment. For example, the system should be energy efficient by consuming as little electricity as possible; for example, equipment should be switched off rather than being left in *stand-by mode* when not in use.

Tasks

1 Karen Stuart has recently opened a sweet shop in the town where she lives. She is considering buying a personal computer to help her run her business. Identify the main start-up and operating costs she is likely to face. If possible, carry out some research to find out how much these items are likely to cost Karen's business.

2 Describe ways in which a new ICT system could minimise its impact on the environment.

3 Carry out some research into the new NHS computer system mentioned above. Assess its impact using the issues covered in this topic.

4 Investigate the ICT systems used by your school or college. How well do they address the issues covered in this topic?

Topic 2.12

Changing business communication systems (1)

Aims

By the end of this topic you should be able to:
- describe the actions which need to be taken to develop and improve business communication systems.

No ICT-based communication system lasts for ever. A system can become out of date and need replacing for a number of reasons including:

- the technology needed to run the system is out of date or cannot be repaired
- the organisation that uses the system now needs to do things the original system wasn't designed for
- the organisation has grown in size and the old system cannot cope with the demands now made of it.

Eventually, all ICT systems need to be improved or replaced. But what needs to happen in order for the new system to be a success? What follows is a list of the main things which need to happen. This is often called the 'systems life cycle' because it describes the stages which a system must go through before it is eventually replaced by a new one.

Plan the improvements

Set objectives for the new system

Objectives are the things the organisation wants the new system to achieve. For example, the

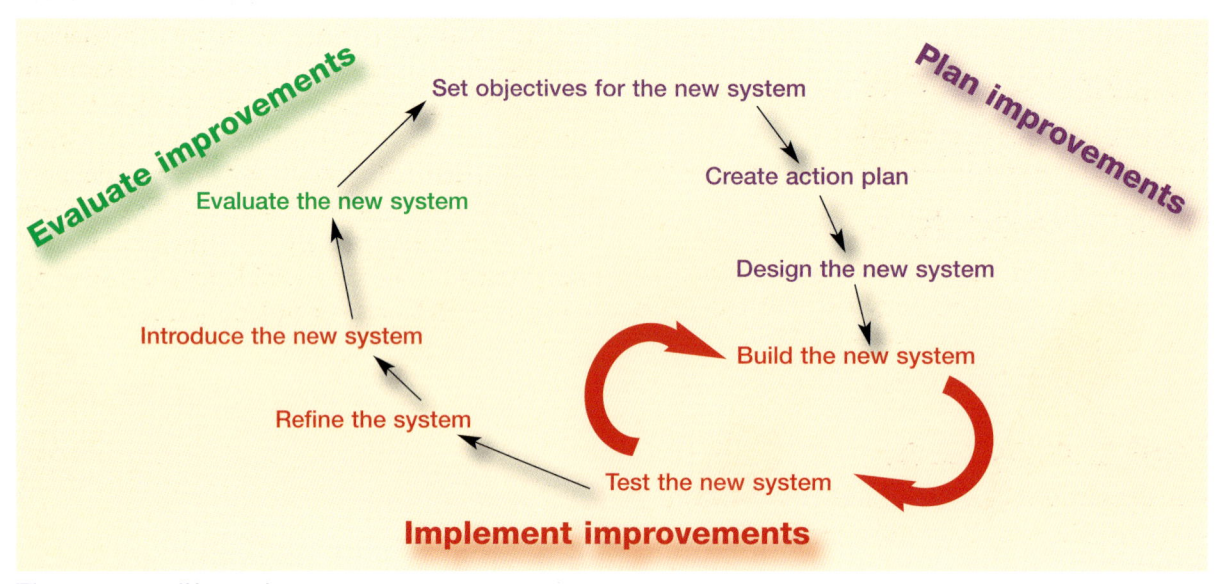

The systems life cycle

objectives for a new website might include:

- must cope with 50,000 visitors a day
- must enable secure online ordering
- must be easy to navigate
- will help increase sales income by 20%.

The objectives will be set by the organisation itself and will relate to the things it wants the system to be able to do and the benefits it will bring to the organisation.

Create an action plan

An action plan sets out how the new system will be created. The plan might include details of:

- actions which need to be taken, e.g. purchase and install software
- deadlines
- resources needed to carry out the actions.

Design the system

At this stage a designer works out exactly how the system will work and what is needed to make this happen. The design might include sketches of what the system will look like and what users will see on their monitor as they use it. It will also include details of the hardware needed and how the software will work.

Implement the improvements

Build the system

The completed design is then used to create the system. Hardware and software will either be purchased or specially created and the whole system will be put together.

Test the system

The system will then be tested to make sure it works as planned. Any problems can then be solved.

Refine the system

The results of the tests carried out can be used to make improvements to the system before it is finally completed.

Introduce the system

Once the system is ready it can be introduced and used by the organisation. This might start with staff being trained how to use it before it 'goes live'. Sometimes the old system is switched off when the new one is introduced. Sometimes they will run alongside each other for a time in case there are problems with the new one.

Evaluation of impact

When the system has been operational for a while, its performance can be compared with the objectives that were set. This will usually happen on a regular basis throughout the life of the system. When the system fails to meet these objectives (or when new objectives are set which it cannot meet) then the whole process of designing and implementing an improved system can begin all over again.

Sometimes, things do not always go as planned. In 2008, a new Terminal opened at Heathrow Airport. From the start there were problems with delays, the handling of passenger luggage and the handling of flight information. As a result a number of flights were delayed or cancelled. These problems were caused by the introduction of a new computer system which had not been fully tested prior to introduction, and for which some staff were not fully trained. Some other airports around the world have experienced similar problems introducing computerised luggage-handling systems.

Tasks

1 Put the following stages of the system life cycle into the correct order:
   - test
   - build
   - evaluate
   - refine
   - set objectives
   - design
   - introduce
   - action plan

2 Describe in your own words what happens at each stage of the system life cycle.

3 Why is it important to keep evaluating the performance of an ICT system after it has been successfully introduced?

Topic 2.13

Changing business communication systems (2)

Aims

By the end of this topic you should be able to:
- assess the impact on business organisations and employees of changes to business communication systems.

In the previous topic we looked at what needs to happen when a new ICT-based communication system is introduced. In this topic we will look at some of the consequences of introducing a new system. Some of these consequences will affect the organisation itself and its owners; however, the impact on the other stakeholders is also important.

Financial impact

New systems can be very expensive. Many organisations underestimate both the cost of developing a new ICT system and the time it will take to implement. Disruptions to the introduction of a system can also be expensive; for example, it has been estimated that the cost to British Airways of the problems with the new computer system at Heathrow Airport Terminal 5 in 2005 was over £15 million. There was also disruption to the passengers using the airport, some of whom may have decided not to use it in future.

Training implications

Staff need to be trained how to use a system. This takes time and can be expensive as staff are unable to work whilst they are being trained how to use a system that has not been introduced. The organisation needs to pay the trainers as well as the wages of the staff being trained. The more complex the system, the more training is needed.

Another implication is for any non-business users of the system such as customers using a new website. If they find the new website difficult to use they may go elsewhere.

Changing job roles

The introduction of ICT into organisations over the past thirty years has changed many job roles beyond recognition. For example very few organisations now employ secretaries whose main job is to create documents such as letters for other employees. Many workers in a modern business organisation are now expected to produce their own communications, and they often have the choice over which method to use. They are also expected to be responsible for their own administration, such as saving their computer documents in an organised electronic filing system and managing an electronic diary.

A new system is also an opportunity for employees to learn new skills (this process is called *re-skilling*) or to carry out more than one activity at a time (such as updating their electronic diary whilst talking with a client over the telephone) – this is called *multi-tasking*.

Changing working practices

The development of the internet and the use by many organisations of an *intranet* (see Topic 2.4), as well as the development of communications devices and mobile computing, has led to other changes to working patterns. These include remote working.

Remote working happens when a person is able to carry out productive work whilst away from the office. This could happen whilst they are travelling, or when working from home. There has been a big increase in recent years in the number of people who spend at least part of their working week at home. This has largely been due to the growth of communications technology such as the internet and intranets.

Benefits and drawbacks of working from home:

- less time is spent travelling to and from the office. This time could be spent working (a benefit for the business) or looking after the family (a benefit for the employee)
- the worker will be less tired due to less travelling. This could also result in more productive work
- the business needs less office space as it will have fewer people in the office on any one day
- the worker could easily get distracted by events at home: this might result in less work being done
- it might be harder for the organisation and the worker to keep in contact with each other, resulting in a sense of isolation or loneliness for the worker, and less effective monitoring of performance by the employer.

Redundancies/new employment opportunities

One of the aims of a new system is often to reduce business costs. One way this can be achieved is if the system can perform tasks automatically which previously needed people to carry them out. Redundancy is the term used to describe the process where someone loses their job because their employer no longer needs someone to carry out the work – this is either because the tasks are no longer needed or because a computer is able to perform them instead.

However, computers also help to create work. For example there are many thousands of people employed as web designers, systems engineers, network managers or computer technicians whose jobs did not exist thirty years ago. There are also hundreds of thousands of people employed in e-commerce firms, for example as warehouse operatives. Many of these businesses are less than ten years old.

Tasks

1. State two benefits and two drawbacks to an employee of working from home.
2. Explain two benefits and two drawbacks to a business of having some of its staff working from home.
3. Explain how the development of the internet has affected business organisations and their employees.

Topic 2.14
The controlled assessment

Aims

By the end of this topic you should be able to:
- understand the purpose of controlled assessment
- understand how the controlled assessment is carried out
- understand what will happen during the controlled assessment.

Unit A266 is assessed by a controlled assignment. You will be given a series of tasks to complete. These tasks will require you to investigate the communication systems used by an existing business and make recommendations for how they are to be improved.

In order to complete the tasks you will need to carry out some research. You will be given a set amount of time to complete your research. Your answers to the tasks will be given under the supervision of a teacher and there will be controls on what you can and cannot do (for example you cannot discuss or share your work with other students).

You will have approximately ten hours to carry out your research (this could be spread over a number of days or even weeks) and approximately five hours to complete the tasks.

An example of a controlled assignment is given below.

Example Controlled Assignment

The owner of a local shop has asked you to investigate how the business communicates with its customers.

The owner has given you the following terms of reference.

I would like you to investigate the ways in which our shop communicates with its customers and make recommendations for how our systems and/or communications can be improved. You should present your work to me as a formal business report. You will have up to ten hours in which to design, carry out and analyse research for this project and up to five hours to produce your written report and letter.

The specific requirements for the report and letter are given in Tasks 1 and 2 below.

Tasks

Task 1

Your report should contain answers to the following.

(a) Describe the main features of the communication systems the shop uses to communicate with customers. (6 marks)

(b) Describe the main messages and media which the shop uses to communicate with customers. (6 marks)

(c) Analyse the capabilities and limitations of the existing systems used by the shop to communicate with customers. (6 marks)

(d) What do customers think of the communications received from the shop and what recommendations for improvement do they make? Why do they want these improvements to take place?
(6 marks)

(e) What recommendations would you make for improvements in the way in which communication takes place between the shop and its customers? Explain why you are making these recommendations.
(6 marks)

(f) What impact will these changes have on the shop and its customers? Why is this?
(9 marks)

The report can be word-processed and should be of professional quality including appropriate charts, graphs, graphics, images, tables and a bibliography. You should use a structure appropriate to a formal report.
(6 marks)

Task 2

Produce a high-quality letter which the owner can use to persuade customers to accept the changes you propose. The letter should emphasise the benefits to customers of the proposed changes.
(15 marks)

(Total: 60 marks)

You might choose to investigate a shop which has a website, in which case you could look at its website to see if there are ways in which it could be improved. One improvement might be to have space for each branch to include more details about itself, e.g. location, special offers, contact details etc. The shop might not have a website, in which case you might consider whether it should introduce one.

You might have seen an advertisement by the shop in a local newspaper, in which case you could investigate whether there are other ways the business could advertise to its customers.

The important thing is that you first study the existing communications systems used by the shop. You should then ask customers about the existing communications and whether they have any suggested improvements. Finally, you should make your own recommendations for how the shop could improve the way it communicates with customers.

Note that Task 1 asks you to produce a formal business report and Task 2 a letter. You should aim to use no more than 2000 words when completing these two tasks. We will look at these documents in the next section.

The controlled assignment changes every year. However Task 1 will always be to produce a formal business report. This was covered in Topic 2.3. The document for Task 2 changes each year and can be either a slideshow presentation, a web-page, a letter or a leaflet. Unit A267 explores in more detail the purpose of these documents and how they can be produced.

UNIT 3

ICT SKILLS FOR BUSINESS COMMUNICATION SYSTEMS

Unit 3: ICT Skills for Business Communication Systems

Topic 3.1a

> Producing straightforward business documents using a word processor (business letters)

Aims

By the end of this topic you should be able to:
- describe what a business letter is
- explain the importance of a well-written business letter
- create a business letter in the fully blocked style, using open punctuation.

A business letter is a formal type of letter usually used as a form of communication from business to business and between businesses and their customers. The software used to create this type of document is called word processing software.

A business letter is written in a special style. This style is called the 'fully blocked style' and uses what is known as 'open punctuation'. It is important that business letters always follow this style as it would give a poor impression of the business if an incorrect style was used; this may make customers think the business is unprofessional.

The fully blocked style is where each line begins to the left of the margin. Open punctuation means that punctuation is only used in the body of the letter, nowhere else.

Business letter layout
Letter head
Reference (if necessary)
Date
Name (if available)
Address and postcode
Salutation
Body of letter
Complimentary close
Signature
Name, position
ENC (if necessary)

Rules for the salutation and complimentary close

If you write to Dear Mr Jones, you must close the letter with Yours sincerely.

If you write to Dear Sir/Madam, you must close the letter with Yours faithfully.

Explanation

(1) The letter head is usually placed at the top of the letter. This will include the contact details of the business and usually the business's logo. Businesses will have this saved as a template so staff can re-use it every time they want to write a new letter.

If there is a *(2)* reference, this should be put at the top of the letter.

Then the *(3)* date.

Next goes the *(4)* recipient's name.

Producing straightforward business documents using a word processor (business letters)

The Florist

Web: theflorist.co.uk
email: contact@theflorist.co.uk
Tel 0121 827191
Fax 0121 827192

The Florist
17 King Street
Cardiff
CF51 8UJ

1. Letter head

Ref: 98102/09   **2. Reference**

17 July 2008   **3. Date**

Mr Harold Rees   **4. Recipient's name**
Sunny Hotel
29 Mountain Road   **5. Recipient's address and postcode**
Swansea
SA1 2JU

Dear Mr Rees   **6. Salutation**

Thank you for getting in touch with us about placing an ongoing order for various seasonal flower arrangements for your hotel and the possibility of a discount.

I am pleased to inform you that we will be able to offer you a business discount. This discount will depend on the amount of flowers you require and how often you place the order. It is important at this stage for you to meet with one of our sales representatives to discuss this further. Could you attend our Head Office on Monday 21 July at 9.00 am?

Could you please contact me to confirm your attendance at this meeting. I have enclosed a map to help you find our location.

7. Body of the letter

Yours sincerely   **8. Complimentary close**

J. Harries   **9. Signature**

Joanne Harries
Assistant Manager   **10. The person's name and position**

ENC   **11. Items enclosed**

A business letter

Then the *(5)* recipient's address and postcode as shown.

Next the *(6)* salutation. This will either be *Dear* … then the person's name or *Dear Sir/Madam* … if the name is unknown.

Because we are using open punctuation, no commas, full stops etc. should be used up to this point.

The *(7)* body of the letter refers to the content of the letter. It is good practice to use at least three paragraphs if possible. In this section punctuation is used as normal.

To end the letter, use the *(8)* complimentary close. You will use *Yours sincerely* if you know the person's name in your salutation or *Yours faithfully* if you used *Dear Sir/Madam* in your salutation, if you don't know the recipient's name.

Next is the person's *(9)* signature. This is usually signed later after printing so a space of about five lines should be left to make space for this when word-processing.

(10) The person's name and position should be typed as shown.

If anything is included with the letter 'ENC' should be added to represent *(11)* items enclosed, then the item enclosed should be named.

Tasks

1. a Describe what a business letter is.

   b Explain what the terms 'fully blocked style' and 'open punctuation' mean.

2. Read the following business letter which contains several mistakes. List as many as you can.

Green Arrow Recruitment

Green Arrow Recruitment
17 Dew Road
Coventry
CV2 7UJ

Web: green_arrowrecruitment.com
email: jobs@green_arrowrecruitment.com

Tel: 024 82930311
Fax: 024 82930512

Mrs Sandra Millany,
2 Queen's Street,
Coventry,
CV6 8UY.

Dear Mrs Millany,

Ref: SM/200808

Thank you for joining our recruitment agency. We have been busy looking for a suitable job for you from the details we have about you. However, there are a few more details we need to know.

We know that you are interested in bar work. However, we need to know if you are looking for full time or part time work. We also need to know how far you are willing to travel to work and whether you have your own transport. Lastly, could you let us know if there is any other type of work that interests you.

Could you please write back to us with these details as this will help us to find you a suitable job.

Yours faithfully

D. Sullivan

Debbie Sullivan
Manager

---

3. Word-process a reply to the letter. You are Sandra Millany. Let Debbie Sullivan know you are interested in part-time work; you will travel; and have your own car. Also let her know you are also interested in restaurant work as well. Ask her to send you details of suitable jobs as soon as possible. Say you have enclosed a copy of your updated C.V.

Quick thought

Why is it so important that businesses follow this particular style of writing business letters?

Topic 3.1b

▶ Producing straightforward business documents using a word processor (memoranda)

Aims

By the end of this topic you should be able to:
- describe what a memorandum is
- explain what house style is
- create a professional-quality memorandum.

A memorandum (or memo for short) is a type of formal communication used by businesses to communicate within the business. Memos are usually short messages that can be sent to one person or groups of people. A letter head or logo is not required but a business may use a template so all the memos look the same, following the business's 'house style'.

Look at the example of a memo below. It is much more informal than the business letter in style.

'To' indicates who the memo is being sent to.

'From' indicates who is writing the memo.

'Date' is the date on which the memo was written.

'Subject' refers to what the memo is about.

There is no need to sign a memo, use salutation or complimentary close.

Example of a memo
Memorandum
To: Sidad Hussain
From: Tina Thomas
Date: 18.08.08
Subject: Performance review
Please could you meet with me for your performance review next Monday in my office at 10.00 am. Please confirm you are able to attend the meeting and also provide your sales figures for the last quarter.
Thanks

Research task

Imagine you are Sidad and word-process a memo in reply to the one above. Tell Tina you are unable to make the meeting because you have another meeting at that time. Ask if it is possible to re-arrange for the same time and place the following day. Confirm you have your sales figures ready.

Quick thought

Memos have been replaced by email in many businesses. What are the advantages and disadvantages of this?

House Style

House style is the style adopted by a business that everyone uses when writing documents. The house style will define the way that information is presented. For example it might include details of:

- text formatting including font styles and sizes
- colours to use as backgrounds and in text (these will match the corporate colours)
- preferred transitions and animations when creating slide show presentations
- position of logo on documents.

A house style helps to ensure that all communications produced by the business have a consistent style. This will help customers to recognise who the communication is from and help to strengthen its *corporate image*.

Tasks

1 Collect at least two different documents from the same organisation. Try to identify what is consistent about the appearance of the documents. Use this information to create a house style for the business.

2 Imagine that you work for the business. The manager thinks it is time the house style was updated. Create a new house style for the business.

Topic 3.1c

Producing straightforward business documents using a word processor (documents for a formal business meeting)

Aims

By the end of this topic you should be able to:
- describe what a Notice of Meeting is
- describe what an Agenda is
- describe the 'standard' and 'non-standard' items on an Agenda
- create a Notice of Meeting and an Agenda.

Notice of Meeting and Agenda

To let staff know a meeting will be held a Notice of Meeting and Agenda will be produced and distributed. This is a type of invitation to a meeting. It also lets everyone know what is to be discussed in the meeting and any other details they need to know. The Notice of Meeting and Agenda can be two separate documents, or they can be combined into a single document.

Notice of Meeting

This is a word-processed document that is distributed to everyone who is invited to the meeting. It will tell them the date, time and venue of the meeting. This document is usually only a few lines long and will include the names of the people invited to the meeting.

Agenda

An Agenda is a word-processed document telling everyone invited to the meeting exactly what will be discussed. It also gives attendees an opportunity to prepare for the meeting. An Agenda follows a particular pattern, including *standard items* that must be used every time an Agenda is produced. These are as follows:

- apologies for absence
- minutes of last meeting
- matters arising
- correspondence.

The *main business* is where the items that will be discussed in the meeting are listed. These change every meeting; they are *non-standard items*.

- any other business (AOB)
- details of next meeting.

> A Notice of Meeting and Agenda are usually distributed to staff as one document, as seen on the next page. In an exam you will usually be asked to produce these as one document; however it is important to know what goes into each part!

Explanation of items on an Agenda

During the meeting the *Chair* will lead the meeting by going through the items on the Agenda.

- Apologies for absence: This is where the people who could not attend the meeting are listed.

- Minutes of last meeting: The minutes of the previous meeting are given to everyone; they all read these minutes and everyone should agree that these are correct.

- Matters arising: Once everyone has read the minutes from the last meeting, any 'matters arising' or anything to report back from these minutes is discussed.

- Correspondence: Any relevant letters that have been received are then discussed if necessary.

- The main business: This is a list of items relating to that particular meeting to be discussed. This could be any number of items and can be about any topic.

- Any other business (AOB): This is where people in the meeting are given a chance to raise any issues they want to.

- Details of next meeting: This is where the date, time and venue of the next meeting, if known, are confirmed.

> **Notice of Meeting**
>
> A meeting will be held for all Sales Staff in the Conference Suite on Friday 22 August 2008 at 10.00 am.
>
> Agenda
>
> 1. Apologies for absence
> 2. Minutes of last meeting
> 3. Matters arising
> 4. Correspondence
> 5. Sales figures for July
> 6. Sales targets for September
> 7. New product promotion
> 8. Any other business
> 9. Details of next meeting.

Which are the non-fixed items in this Agenda?

Definition

The minutes of a meeting are a written record of what was said in a meeting. One person is given the job of taking notes and recording what was said. Why is it important that minutes are written?

Tasks

1. Why is it important that a Notice of Meeting is given to all staff?

2. Imagine you are the Head's PA in your school. He/she would like you to prepare a Notice of Meeting and Agenda for a staff meeting to be held in the school hall at 4.30 on 12 October. You must include the standard items and the following non-standard items on your document

   - Year 10 school trip
   - Refurbishment of the school canteen
   - Mock exam timetable

3. Explain why you think it is important that all meetings follow the Agenda structure.

Topic 3.1d

Producing straightforward business documents using a word processor (documents for a training/conference event)

Aims

By the end of this topic you should be able to:
- describe what a training/conference programme is
- create the layout of a training/conference programme.

Conference

A conference is an event organised by a business or many businesses to discuss issues relating to that type of business. There are often various events and speakers. There is usually a programme or timetable of events in a conference so that each member knows where to go and at which time.

Training

Staff in a business are often given ongoing training to make sure they have up-to-date skills and knowledge. This can often be in the form of a training event where, like in a conference, a programme or timetable of training is drawn up.

Training/conference programme

Word processing software is used to draw up a timetable of events at conferences or training days. Tables are often used to break up the slots, times and venues. Breaks for coffee and lunch are also specified. Very often, attendees can pick and choose from several events.

Example of a conference programme

Mobile phone conference 2008		
9.00 am to 9.30 am	Coffee served in the Main Canteen	
9.30 am to 10.30 am	New product demonstration in the Conference Hall	Motivating Sales Staff talk in the Business Centre
10.30 am to 11.00 am	Coffee served in the Main Canteen	
11.00 am to 12.30 pm	Guest speaker – Speech 'The Future of Mobile Phones' in the Business Centre.	New product demonstration in the Conference Hall
12.30 pm to 1.30 pm	Lunch in the Dining Suite	
1.30 pm to 3.00 pm	Contract Management talk in the Business Centre	Guest speaker – Speech 'Mobile Phone Competition' in the Conference Hall.

Tasks

1 Create a programme for the following event:

Noble Chairs Limited is holding a training day for all their sales staff. It is to be held at the City Hotel, Coventry on January 15th. The event will start at 10.00 am but delegates can arrive from 9.30 am onwards when coffee will be available. There will be four one-hour sessions. There will be one coffee break in the morning and one in the afternoon. Lunch will also last one hour. In addition there will be an introduction at 10.00 am lasting 15 minutes and there will be a similar closing session at the end of the day.

Topic 3.2

Creating simple images and logos using graphics software

Aims

By the end of this topic you should be able to:
- describe the main features of graphics software
- explain the advantages and disadvantages of graphics software
- create a logo using graphics software.

Graphics are used to enhance the appearance of things such as books, magazines and packaging. The most common type of graphic you will see are logos: these help you recognise organisations quickly. You can use graphics software to create simple images and logos. It can also be used to edit photos.

Features of graphics software

Resizing

Images can easily be made larger or smaller by dragging them with the mouse. It is important that when images are resized it is done from the corner of the image, otherwise the image will be distorted.

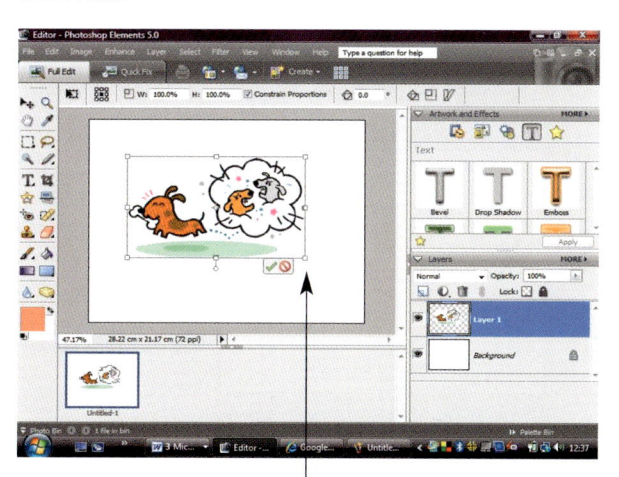

Resize image from the corner

Cropping

You can remove parts of the graphic by cropping.

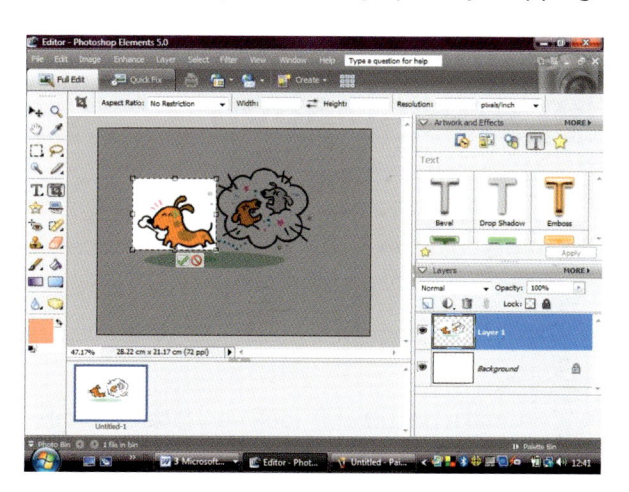

Editing

You can change colours in images to change their appearance.

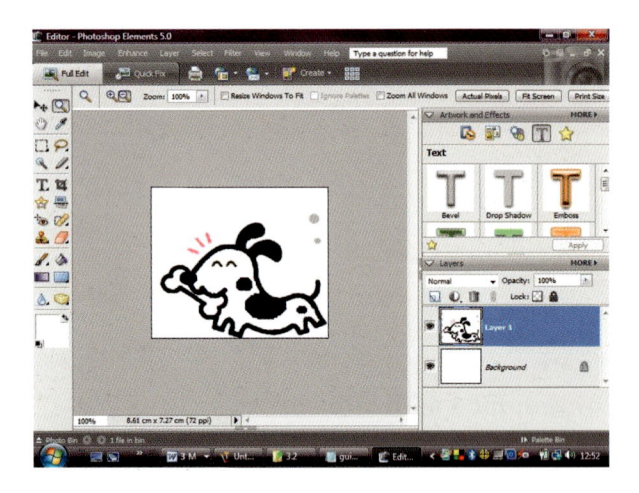

Quick thought

Brand image is where a business builds up a brand that is very recognisable. This is done through using a consistent theme on all of its products and documents. If you saw the logo of a business with good brand image you would immediately associate this with the business's products or services. Why is it important for an organisation to develop "Brand image"?

Creating logos

1. Draw the three shapes as shown here.

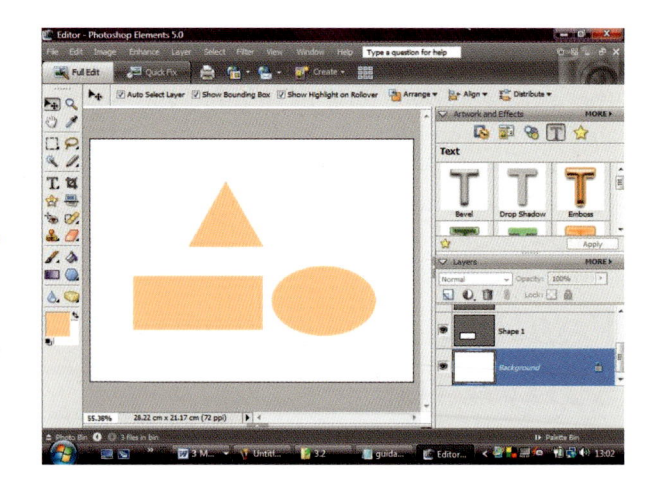

2. Rearrange the shapes as shown and flatten the image.

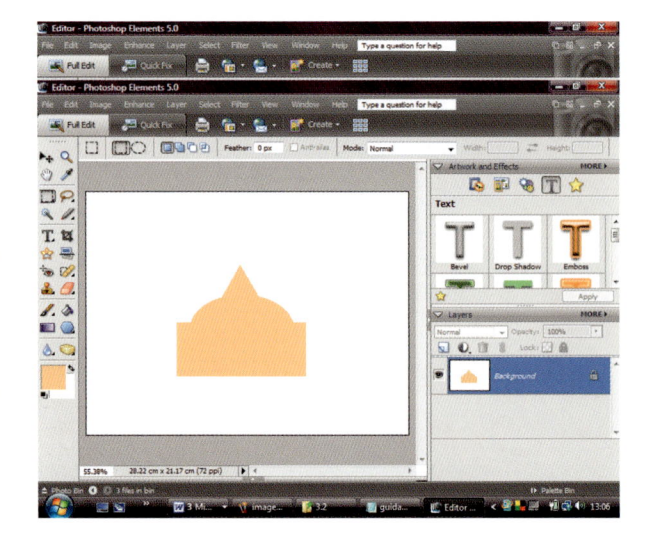

Advantages and disadvantages of graphics software to an organisation

Benefits

- Numerous features available to create professional images and graphics.
- Can create original, copyright-free logos and images.
- Can make documents look very professional.
- Can help an organisation develop 'Brand Image'.

Drawbacks

- Professional graphics software is expensive.
- Can be difficult to use.
- Lots of complex features.
- Training will be necessary, which can be expensive.
- Can be very time-consuming to use.
- Need a high-specification computer to run the software.

3. Use the filter tools available to change the block colour to a suitable finish.
4. Use the text tool to find a suitable font and write the name of the organisation.

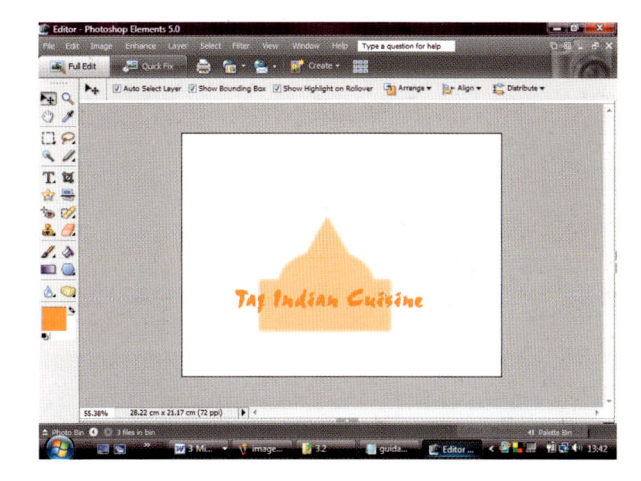

Tasks

1. You are the assistant manager of Taj Indian Cuisine. The manager is considering buying graphics software. He wants you to investigate the advantages and disadvantages before he makes his final decision. Write a report advising him on this.

2. Recreate the logo for Taj Indian Cuisine.

3. Use the logo to create a letter head for Taj Indian Cuisine.

Topic 3.3

❯ Creating complex business documents using Desk Top Publishing software

Aims

By the end of this topic you should be able to:
- describe what Desk Top Publishing software is
- explain the various features of Desk Top Publishing software
- create various complex business documents using Desk Top Publishing software.

In order to create professional-looking leaflets, brochures, posters, newsletters, business cards and many other documents, the best software to use is Desk Top Publishing software (DTP). Many of the features of DTP software are available in Word Processing Software, but it is much easier in DTP software to work with images, adapt layouts and control the number of pages.

Features of DTP software

Templates
DTP software supplies lots of ready-made templates, like posters, leaflets etc., that have been professionally laid out with graphics and formatting; these can then be edited to suit whatever the DTP task.

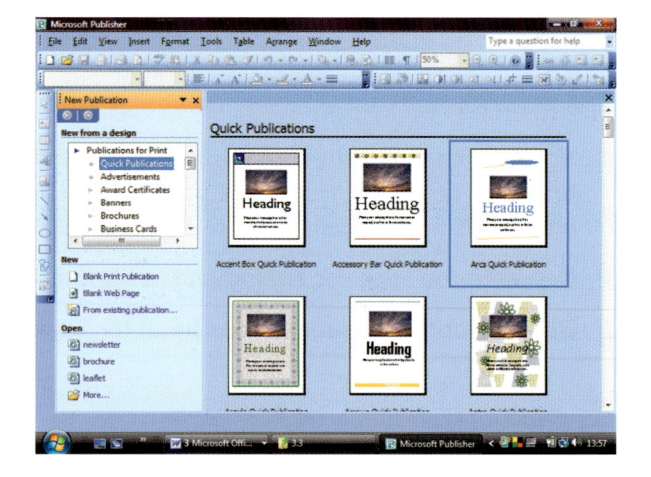

Toolbar
The toolbar is always available and allows users to find features quickly.

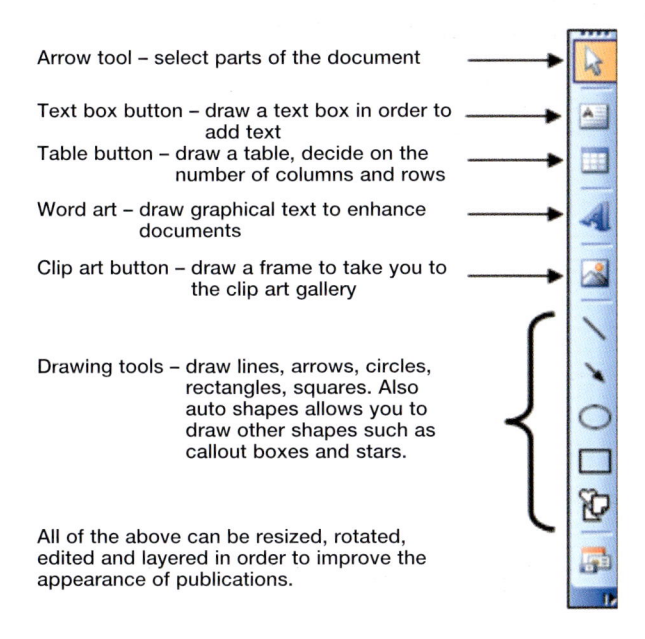

Creating complex business documents using Desk Top Publishing software

Arrow tool – select parts of the document

Text box button – draw a text box in order to add text

Table button – draw a table, decide on the number of columns and rows

Word art – draw graphical text to enhance documents

Clip art button – draw a frame to take you to the clip art gallery

Drawing tools – draw lines, arrows, circles, rectangles, squares. Also auto shapes allows you to draw other shapes such as callout boxes and stars.

All of the above can be resized, rotated, edited and layered in order to improve the appearance of publications.

The toolbar

Quick thought

Think of some of the people or organisations that may use DTP software. What sort of publications would they create?

Colour schemes

The colour scheme option allows the user to easily change the colour of a document, using colours that work well together.

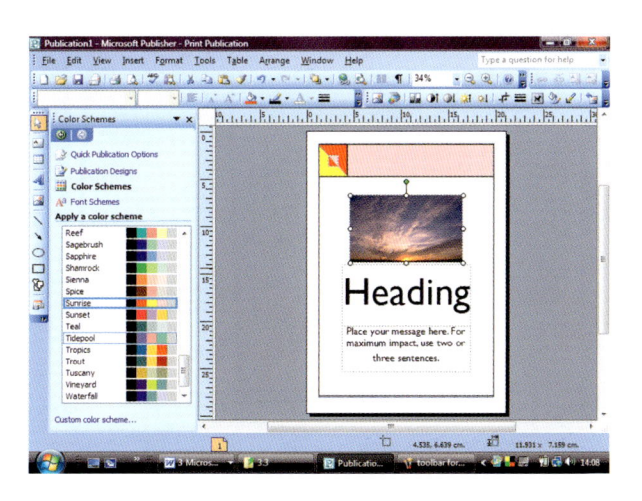

Tabs

The tab option allows the user to flick between pages in documents that have more than one page. The page that the user is working on is highlighted.

Other features

Other features of DTP software include:

- layering – images and text can be sent in front and behind each other easily
- fonts – various font sizes and styles can be selected
- wizards – make it easy to customise templates
- frames – can be used to construct pages
- wrap text – makes text wrap around images
- borders – various custom borders make it easy to enhance documents.

The advantages and disadvantages of using DTP software

Benefits
- High-quality documents can be produced easily.
- No need to employ an expensive designer.
- High-quality professional documents improve the image of the business.
- Wizards and templates allow non-expert staff to create documents quickly and easily.

Drawbacks
- Software can be expensive to purchase.
- A high-quality printer is needed to print the documents to get the full effect.
- A high-specification computer is needed to run the software.
- Staff may require expensive training in order to fully use all features.

Creating business documents using DTP software

One of the documents that a business may create using DTP software is a brochure. Brochures may be used to advertise something in detail. Text and images would normally be combined to give the customer details of products and prices. Alternatively, brochures could even be given to staff to inform them about new policies in the workplace.

To create a brochure in DTP software, you have a few options. You can create a document from scratch: this will make your document different from the rest and, if done well, will look professional. However, it can end up looking unprofessional if too many or not enough DTP features are used, or if the creator is not familiar with the software.

Another option is to use one of the many templates on offer. These produce professional documents quickly. However, it can be obvious to the audience that the document has been created using a template: this is mainly because they are used so often that they have become very familiar. There are a few things you can do to enhance the appearance of the templates and make them look more unique.

Creating your document

Open your DTP software and select *Publications for Print*, then select *Brochure*. There are various options to choose from. Make your selection considering the audience and purpose of the document.

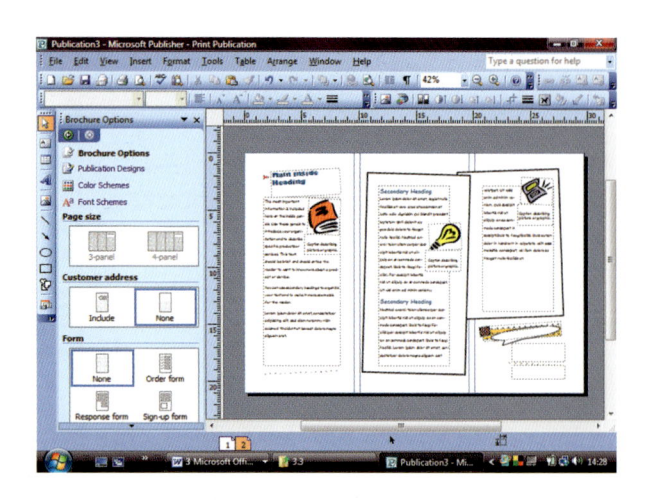

The tabs will be used to flick between the front and back of the brochure.

This is what the template might look like; the text can be replaced with suitable information. Also, the images can be replaced with suitable images.

A good way to customise the template is to make the features available more dramatic. This can be done by filling frames with colour and by making borders thicker. If the template has provided you with some shapes for design purposes, make them bigger by clicking on them and stretching them with the mouse.

As for a colour scheme, the best advice is to keep to a few colours. Perhaps match the colours to the main colours in a picture or a logo. All these features are shown below:

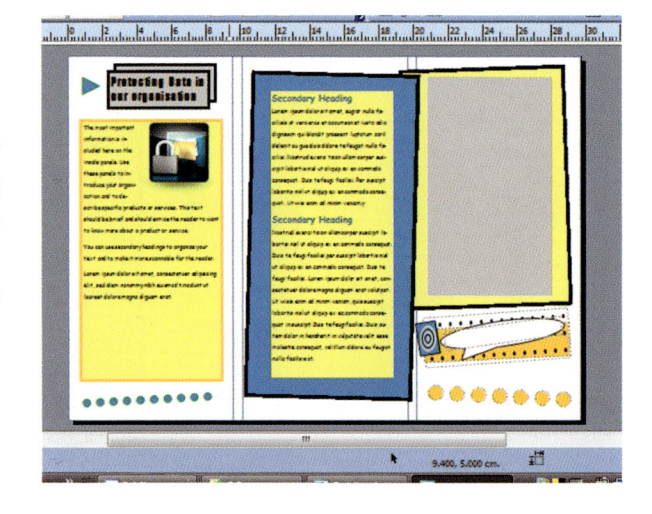

Creating complex business documents using Desk Top Publishing software 135

Filling colour

Click on whatever object is to be edited. White dots will appear around the object selected. Then click on the *fill* tool on the main toolbar to select a suitable colour.

This will then give you further options to choose a suitable colour. Remember to keep colours as light as possible: they tend to look darker when printed than they do on screen.

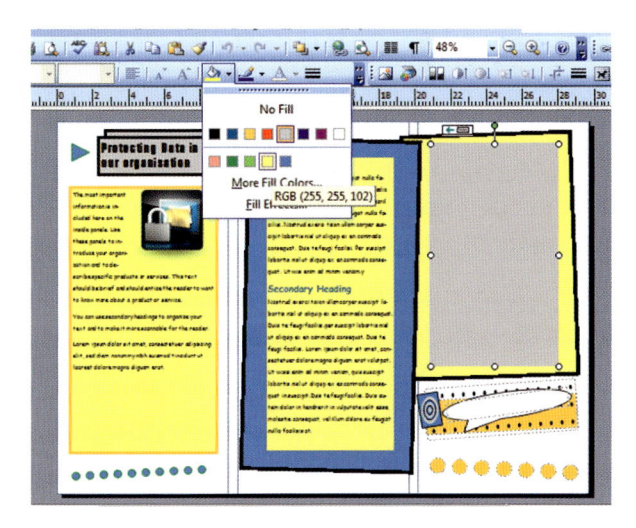

Borders

Another feature that makes a document look more professional is borders. Change the colour and thickness for a more dramatic effect: this can make work stand out and give a professional finish.

Again click on the object a border is to be added to. Firstly change the line colour. Click on the *line colour* tool: it is usually next to the fill colour tool on the main toolbar. As before choose a suitable colour for the border.

The border will look better if it is made thicker. This can be done by selecting the *line/border style* tool on the main toolbar. Then select the thickness of the border for the object. Select more lines to get more styles available, but be careful not to overuse features

Borders can be made more eyecatching by using border art. Using the same process as adding a border, more lines and border art can be selected. Again, be careful not to overuse this feature and keep images relevant.

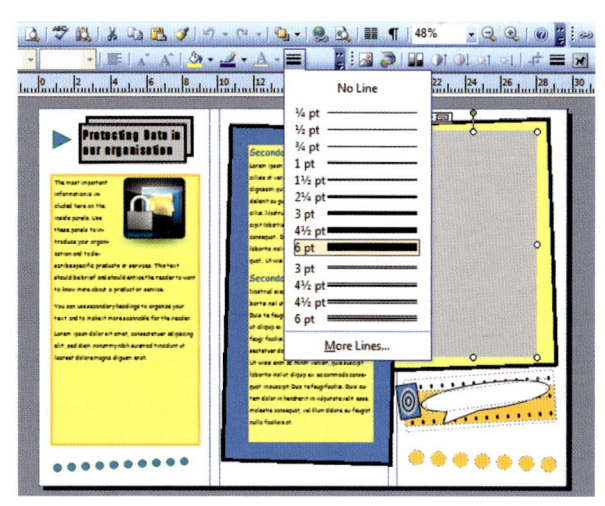

Quick task

Use your skills to improve the appearance of a template in DTP software.

Creating newsletters using DTP software

Another document used by businesses to communicate information with its employees is a newsletter. It will let people know of any events that are happening.

This type of document is usually created using DTP software. There are also templates available to help you give a professional finish to this type of document.

As with a brochure, start a new DTP document and then choose *Publications for Print;* from the option list choose a suitable newsletter template.

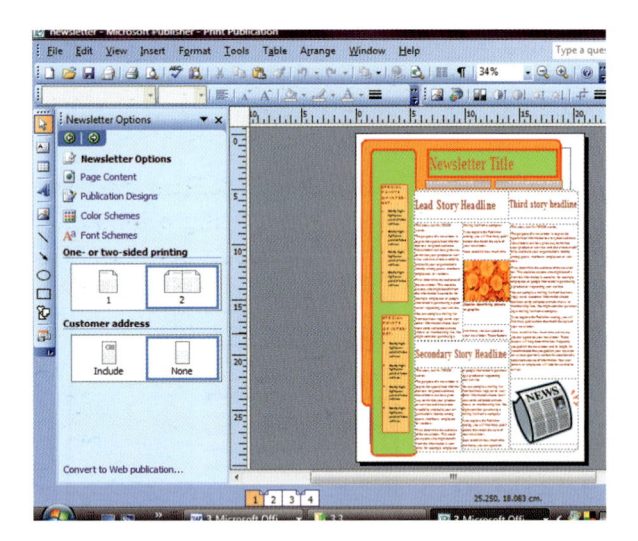

Use the colour scheme options or other techniques to improve the appearance of your document.

Replace the images and text with the information for a newsletter. Use features such as word art, clip art, auto shapes and tables to help communicate information. However, be careful not to overuse features and make it look unprofessional. Also, try to keep to a colour scheme and match the colours to your logo or images as much as possible.

Zooming

A common mistake made when using DTP is to make the font too big. The document that you are working on will automatically appear so you can see the whole document on screen; however, when you print it, it will be much larger. The mistake people often make is to make the font bigger instead of zooming into the document.

By clicking on the *zoom in* tool on the main toolbar this will make the document a more realistic size. *Zoom out* to view the whole document and examine the layout.

Text size for blocks of information should not be bigger than a size 14 and more suitably size 12, otherwise you will not have enough space for all your information and it will look unprofessional.

Quick tip

It is a good idea to use the print preview option at regular intervals. The document tends to look a little plainer in the print preview view when you can't see the outline of all your frames.

Working with columns

Newsletter information is often arranged into columns. This allows you to break up different types of information under different headings.

To make better use of space add more columns as shown below. This can be done by simply moving items by dragging them with the mouse and then creating more text boxes to add more information.

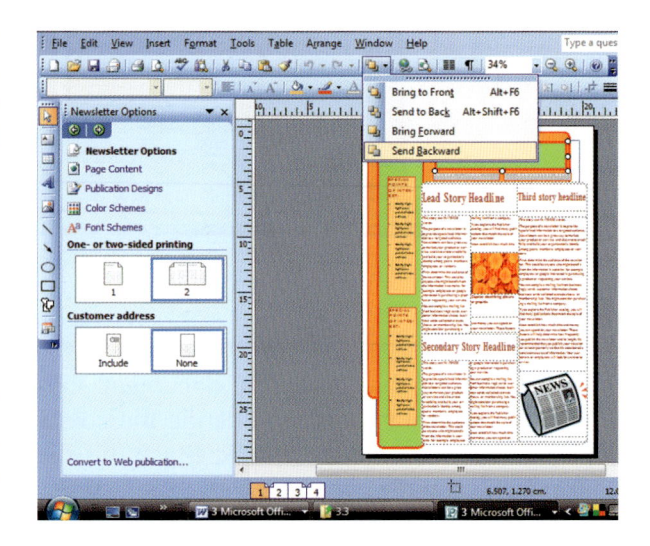

Frames and layering

All DTP documents consist of frames. Whether it is an image, a shape or a text box, these are known as frames. These frames can be layered: on the above document some frames are at the front and others are behind.

To change the layerings of an object use the *layering* tool on the main toolbar. Click on the object to layer, then send the object to the front or back. This can also be done by right clicking with the mouse.

Tasks

1. Your teacher would like you to create a brochure aimed at teachers in your school. The brochure will explain to them about DTP software. Your document should be created using a template; you should use the techniques discussed previously to improve the appearance of this document. You should include your school logo, if available, and use a suitable colour scheme.

    You must explain the following in your brochure:

    - What is DTP software?
    - What are the features of the software?
    - What are the advantages and disadvantages of the software?
    - What impact the use of DTP software could have in the school.

    Add some useful tips for people who are new to using DTP software.

2. Describe to your teacher the features you have used and the changes made to the template.

Topic 3.4

Creating business presentations using presentation software

Aims

By the end of this topic you should be able to:
- describe what presentation software is
- explain the advantages and disadvantages of presentation software
- create a business style presentation using presentation software.

Presentation software is often used in organisations to present ideas to an audience. A business may present the features of a new product to potential customers or the Human Resource Department may train staff using presentation software to display important information. Presentation software is also used at conferences. A large screen and a projector are usually necessary for the presentation.

Features of presentation software

Templates

Presentation software provides lots of professional-looking background templates to enhance the look of a presentation

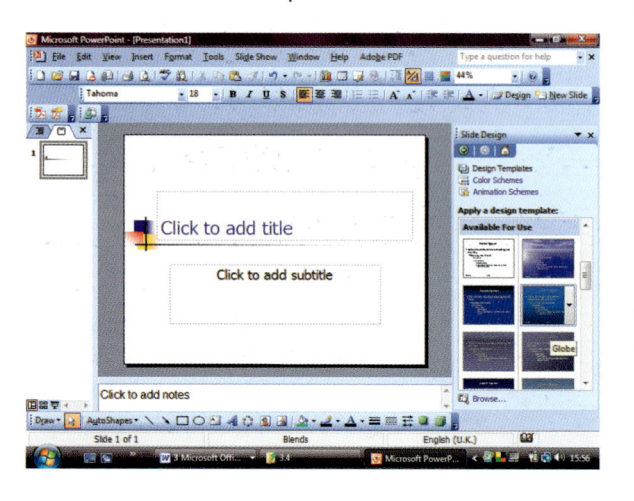

Layout

Presentation software also provides several layouts so slides can be organised in a professional style. Charts, images and even movie clips can be added.

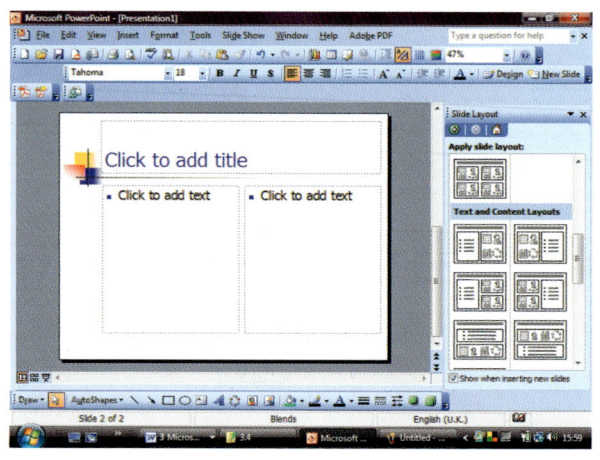

Master Slide

To make a presentation look very professional it is best to keep the same formatting throughout. The Master Slide facility allows you to set this up easily. It can be set up so, for example, a logo, a heading or a style of font will appear on every slide.

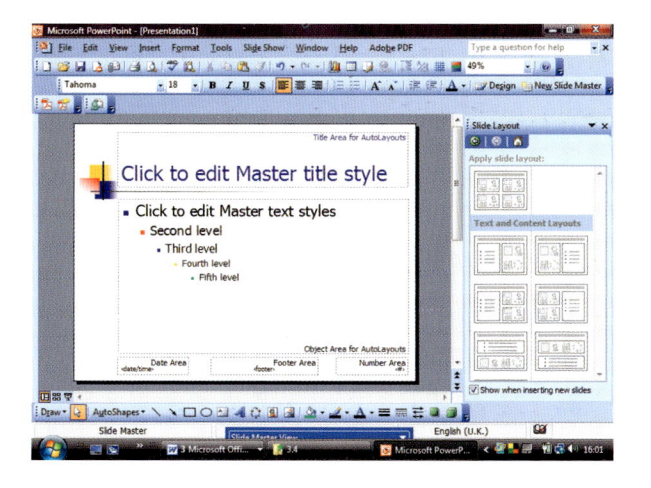

Animations

A presentation can be enhanced with animations. These can be used to emphasise words or simply to hold back information until it is needed.

Timings and voice-overs

There are a few ways a presentation can be presented to the audience: by reading the contents of the slide and explaining concepts further and clicking to go to the next slide as required. Alternatively, timings and even voice-overs can be added, giving the audience sufficient time to read through the information. You can also add a commentary to the slides.

Common mistakes made using presentation software

- Too much information – slide content should be kept to a minimum; the speaker can explain the points further: this can also be done by adding speaker's notes. The main slides should be kept simple with not too much detail.
- Inconsistent formatting – too many colours, fonts or features can make a presentation look unprofessional. A Master Slide helps to keep it simple.
- Overuse of effects – too much or inconsistent animations, unnecessary sounds can result in the audience losing the point of the presentation. Keep it simple.
- Unnecessary images – or overuse of images can make a presentation look too busy and again unprofessional. Keep images to a minimum and make sure they are actually needed and fit for purpose.

Benefits and drawbacks of presentation software

Benefits

- Templates provide professional-looking backgrounds.
- Presentation software is user friendly.
- Effects can improve the impact of the presentation.
- Charts, tables, images and diagrams can help the audience understand the message of the presentation.

Drawbacks

- People often become carried away with the effects available, resulting in an unprofessional presentation.
- Software and hardware can be expensive.
- Training may be needed to use the more complex features of the presentation, which can be expensive.

Important things to remember when creating a business presentation

When creating a business presentation, in order to keep it looking professional, consider the audience will be business people and adults. Remember to:

- keep it simple
- don't overuse effects
- keep the same style throughout the presentation
- keep images, tables, charts and diagrams relevant.

Creating a Master Slide

To create a professional-looking business presentation keep the same sort of formatting throughout i.e. the same style of font and the same background. If possible, add your company logo to every slide and put it in the same place. This can be done by using the Master Slide option. Click *View* on the main toolbar and *Master*, then *Slide Master*.

Formatting can be set from here for the rest of the presentation; for example, slide numbers, font sizes and styles can be added, and backgrounds and logos added as shown below. These will then appear on every slide.

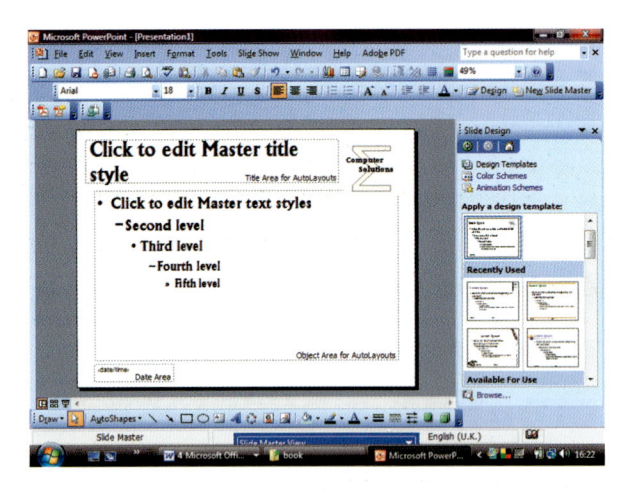

Once the formatting choices have been made, click *Edit* on the main toolbar and select *Preserve Master*, then click *Close Master View*. Slides that are then inserted will include the formatting set up on the Master Slide.

> Why do you think it is important to keep the same style throughout a business presentation?

Adding a chart to your presentation

Numerical data is often better shown in a chart. There are various types of charts available, from column charts to pie charts. It is quite common for a business presentation to include a chart that will then be explained by the speaker.

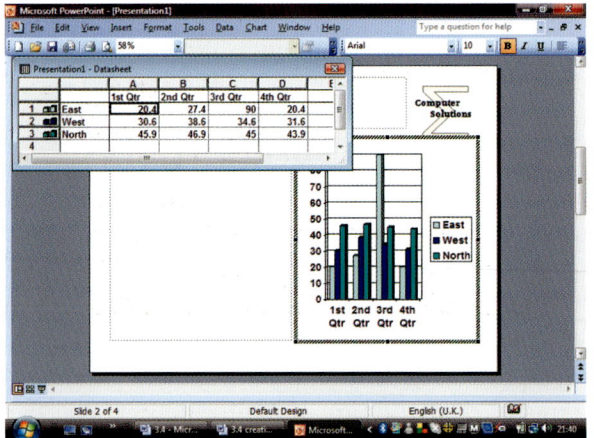

Click *Insert* on the main toolbar and chart. The above page will automatically open. By changing the data in the table with the relevant figures the graph will automatically change. Unwanted columns and rows can easily be deleted by clicking on them and pressing *delete* on the keyboard.

Narration

Sometimes, business presentations are created so people can watch in their own time. In presentation software, narration can be added where people can hear an explanation of each slide. It is necessary to have some sort of microphone attached to the computer. Then on the main toolbar click *Slide Show*, and select *Record Narration*. It will then record the voice and timings ready to be played to the audience.

Effects

It is possible to make a presentation more interesting by adding effects. However, for a business presentation this is more likely to be used to hold back and emphasise information.

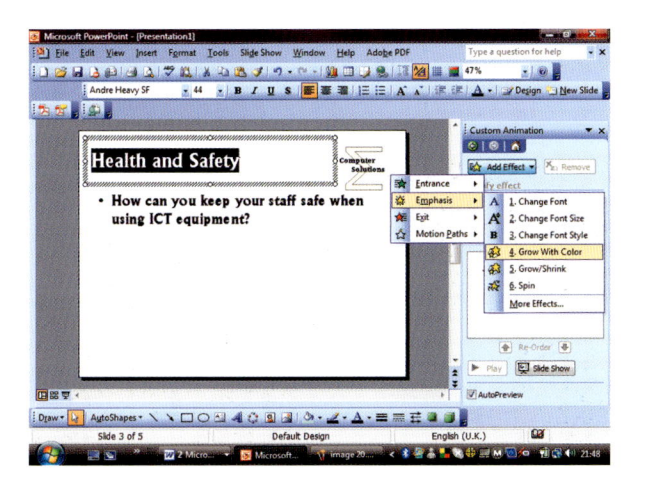

It is possible to get information to enter the screen when specified by the speaker. This will stop the audience reading on and help the speaker to further explain points or it may allow the speaker to pose questions for the audience to think about before releasing the answer.

Quick thought

What sort of impression will an audience receive if effects are overused during a presentation?
Why can narration sometime be a bad idea?

To add effects, go to *Slide Show* on the main toolbar and select *Custom Animation*. Click on the item to be animated and click *Add Effect*.

There are various options available to enhance the presentation. However, in a business presentation these should be kept to a minimum and not too many different styles used or it can end up looking unprofessional.

Tasks

1 You are an IT consultant and have been asked to give a presentation to various business people about presentation software and how it could improve their sales.

You must include the following information:

- what presentation software is
- some of the important features
- the advantages and disadvantages of presentation software to business
- what impact the use of the software could have on sales.

You must include a chart showing the data on the next page. You must also use a Master Slide and add appropriate effects and narration if preferred.

		A	B	C	D
		1st Qtr	2nd Qtr	3rd Qtr	4th Qtr
1	Sales with presentation software	70	80	90	100
2	Sales without presentation software	30.6	38.6	34.6	31.6
3					
4					

2 Once you have completed your presentation, show it to a partner. They must decide if it is a professional-looking business presentation, or if you have overused effects and formatting. Take their advice and change your presentation if necessary.

Topic 3.5

Producing web pages using web creation software

Aims

By the end of this topic you should be able to:
- describe what a web page is
- explain the purpose of a web page for business
- create a simple web page using web design software.

A web page is a page in a website. Web pages can include text, images, video, sound etc. There are many millions of websites on the World Wide Web and these can be accessed by anyone who has an internet connection and a computer.

There are many reasons to have a website. Many Government organisation have websites: their aim is to provide information and possibly some services. For example, the DVLA (Driver and Vehicle Licensing Agency) has a website; this is the UK Government organisation that deals with anything to do with the registration of drivers and vehicles in the UK. Their website is www.dvla.gov.uk: you can get information, buy road tax or even apply for a job.

Charities may have a website: their aim would be to raise awareness, possibly raise funds and give information about their charity. This link shows the Children in Need website: http://www.bbc.co.uk/pudsey/.

Businesses are also likely to have a website. They may just want to advertise their products or services, so when someone searches the internet for their products or services their website will come up and they may get sales. They may use their website to sell their products: this will make their customer base much wider and they will potentially be able to sell to people all over the world.

The structure of a website

A website is usually made up of many pages; the main page that people are likely to go to first is called the home page. The home page will then have links to the other pages on the website.

This is an example of a home page: you can see there are links to other pages and a description of the organisation.

The proper name for the links are *hyperlinks*: a hyperlink is a way of navigating around a website. Hyperlinks are created on words and images: if a word or an image has a hyperlink attached to it, when the mouse goes over it a hand appears, letting the user know that it is a hyperlink. When the user clicks on the link it takes them to another page in the website. The main pages in the web page will usually be displayed in a navigation bar, as seen in our example. Those pages will then have more hyperlinks and more pages attached to them; however, all pages will be linked back to the home page.

Creating websites

Master Slides

There are many types of software available to create a website; whatever software is used, the best method is to create a Master Slide. It is very similar to a Master Slide in presentation software, where it is possible to set up everything you want to appear on every slide. The example below shows a Master Slide: all the colours formatting, links and the banner will appear on every page in the website.

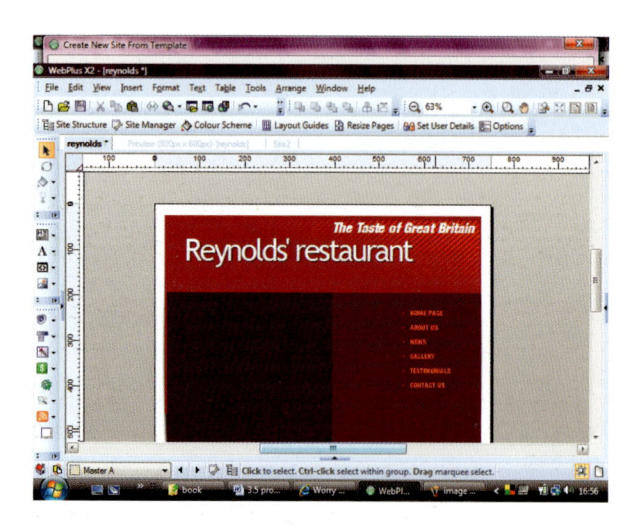

This will also make the website look professional.

Templates

There are also many professional-looking templates available in web design software. As with Desk Top Publishing software, these can be edited to enhance the appearance. It is much easier to use a template, especially in an exam when there is little time. With a template any aspects that are not required can easily be deleted and replaced with more suitable text, images or graphics.

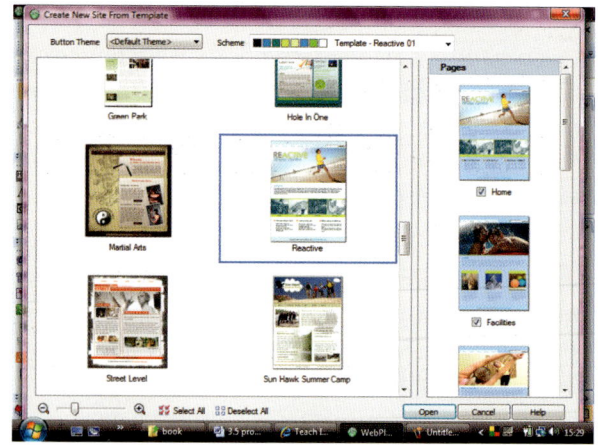

Layout of a web page

It is important that a web page looks like a web page and not like a word-processed document. If there is too much text people will be put off; also too many images may have the same effect. This is an example of how a web page may be laid out: there is a good mixture of images and text and the page is divided into sections. This makes it much easier for the user to read and navigate around.

Producing web pages using web creation software — 145

Banner		
Image	Text	Navigation bar
Text / Text	Image	
	Text	

- People can access information or buy from the business 24 hours a day, seven days a week.
- It is easier and quicker to update a website compared to documentation such as catalogues.
- It could lead to a cut in costs for business: if they start doing more and more business online, less staff will be needed.

Drawbacks

- Designing and maintaining a website can be costly.
- Expert staff are needed to design and maintain the website.
- Technical difficulties can lead to problems.
- Security concerns can be a problem, especially when dealing with people's money or personal details.

Benefits and drawbacks of websites for business

Benefits

- The business will look more professional.
- Potentially, people all over the world can access information on the business or buy its products.

Tasks

1. You are the assistant manager of Odyssey Restaurant. At the moment they don't have a website; you want to convince the manager it would be a good idea to have one.

    Create a four-page website for the restaurant as a sample to show the manager what it could look like. It must include text and graphics. You should create a Master Slide to keep the same style throughout the website. All your pages must be linked.

2. Write a report to the manager explaining the advantages and disadvantages of having a website for the business. You must try and convince him that a website is a good idea for the business by explaining the impact it could have on the business.

Topic 3.6

Analysing numerical information using a spreadsheet

Aims

By the end of this topic you should be able to:
- describe what a spreadsheet is
- explain the various features of a spreadsheet
- create a spreadsheet using a variety of formulae.

A spreadsheet is a piece of software that is used to perform calculations. Many different types of people and organisations use spreadsheets. They are used in business to do a variety of different things such as calculate finances, work with statistics, create graphs and forecast various possibilities. The list of the things that businesses use spreadsheets for is endless. It is a very powerful piece of software. However, it is not that simple to use and there are a few basic things that need to be learned before we start.

As shown below the spreadsheet looks like a grid. It is made up of rectangles known as cells: these cells are made up of columns and rows. Each cell has a unique cell address: we know the address of the cell by finding the column letter and the row number of the cell we are clicked in to.

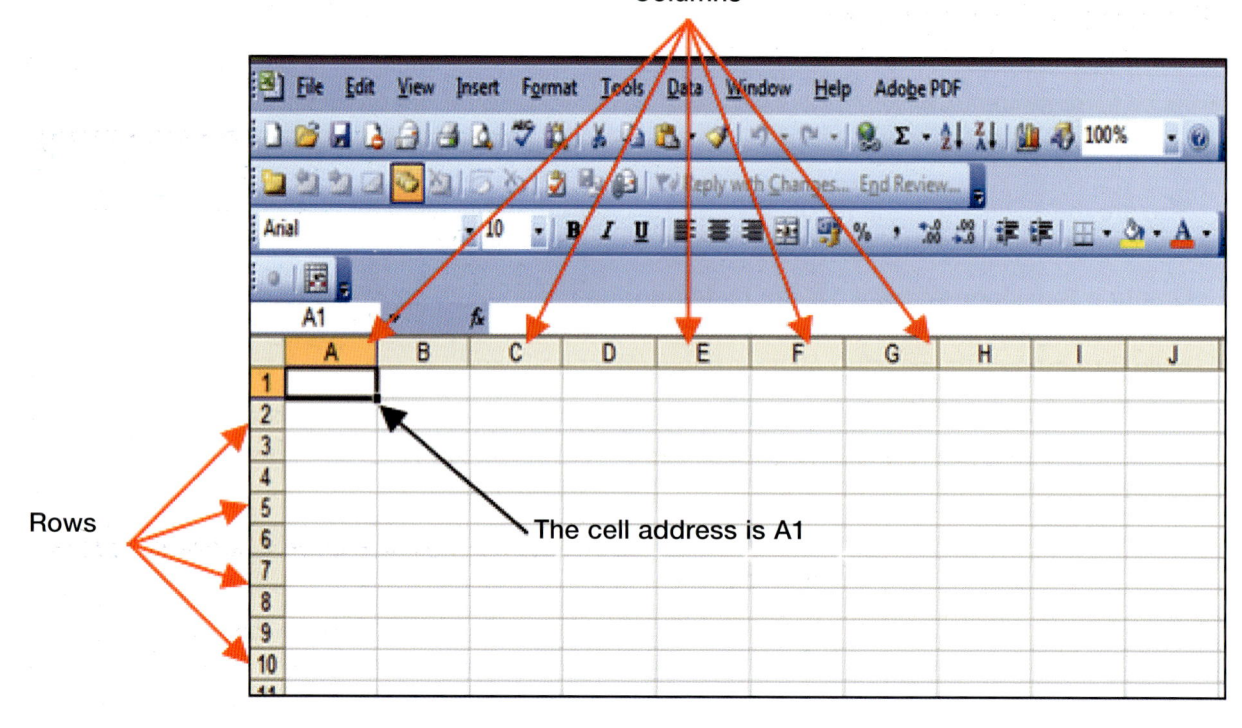

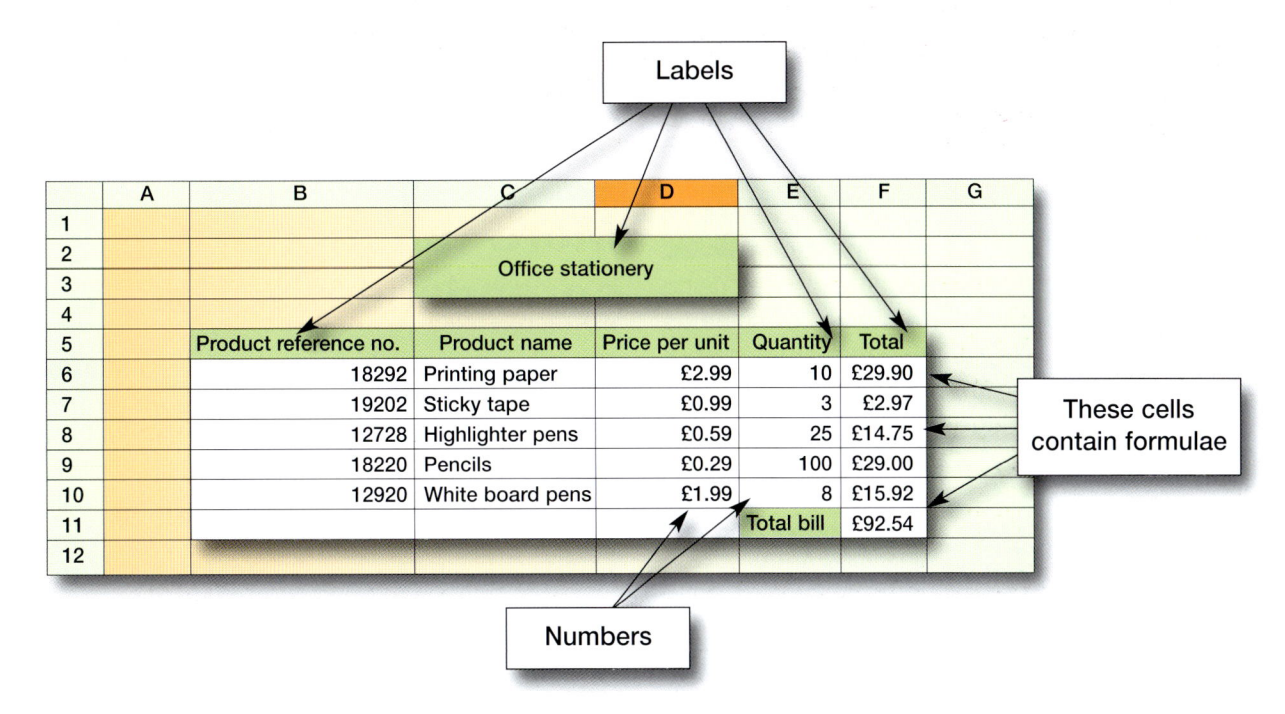

Analysing numerical information using a spreadsheet   147

Labels

	A	B	C	D	E	F	G
1							
2							
3			Office stationery				
4							
5		Product reference no.	Product name	Price per unit	Quantity	Total	
6		18292	Printing paper	£2.99	10	£29.90	
7		19202	Sticky tape	£0.99	3	£2.97	
8		12728	Highlighter pens	£0.59	25	£14.75	
9		18220	Pencils	£0.29	100	£29.00	
10		12920	White board pens	£1.99	8	£15.92	
11					Total bill	£92.54	
12							

These cells contain formulae

Numbers

Text, numbers or formulae can be entered into cells. Text would be in the form of labels. Numbers are what will be calculated and formulae are the instructions you give to the computer to make a calculation.

Simple formulae

To tell the computer to make a calculation a formula must be entered. Click in the cell in which the answer is to appear, then enter the equals sign. A formula must start with the equals sign ' = ': this is how the computer knows it has to calculate something. To multiply two cells, like in the example above, to work out the total for printing paper, click in cell F6, then enter =D6*E6 and then press enter. The answer £29.90 would appear. The sign for multiply is *.

More simple formulae

To create an addition or subtraction formula the signs are the same as you would normally use, '+', '−'. However, to divide use a '/' sign.

Other formulae and functions

To add up a range of cells i.e. two or more cells, there are two options:

either =A1+A2+A3+A4+A5

But to save time, there is a function available called Autosum.

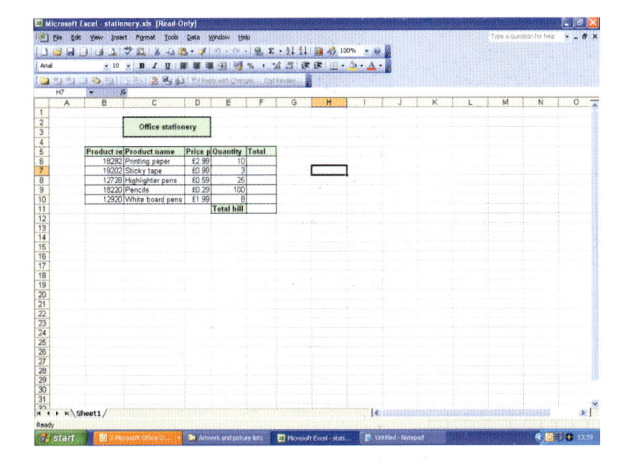

Click where you want the answer to go, then click on the *Autosum* icon Σ and press *enter*. The software will usually automatically recognise the range of cells to add up; if not, the cells to add up can be highlighted while the autosum function is active. The formula will be set up as follows: =SUM(A1:A5): this means add up everything between cells A1 and A5.

Quick task

Recreate the office stationery spreadsheet, using the formulae described. Print your formulae as shown below. Make sure you format your work so it looks fit for purpose: you could add borders, bold headings and fill colour.

Printing your formulae

In an exam when asked to create a spreadsheet, you will always be asked to print your work. However, you must print evidence that you have entered formulae and not just typed in the answers. To do so, click *Tools* on the main toolbar, then choose *Options* and tick *Formulas*.

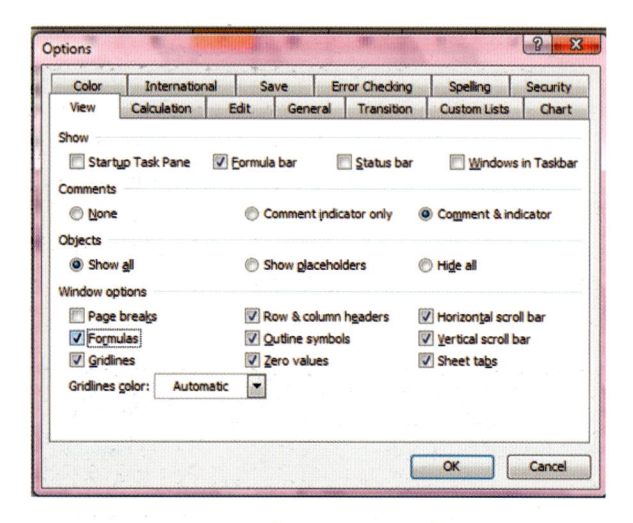

Make sure all formulae can be seen before you print: columns may need adjusting to fit.

Time-saving tip

Save time by copying a formula to other cells. In the office stationery example once you have created your first multiplication formula in cell F6, to save writing the formula over and over again simply highlight cells F6 to F10 and then click *Edit* on the main toolbar, then select *Fill* and *Down*. The spreadsheet will automatically copy the formula.

More functions of spreadsheet software

The above time-saving tip can help stop mistakes. This type of function is called *relative cell referencing*. Basically if there is a formula in cell C1 to add cells A1 and B1 (=A1+B1), and it was copied down to the next cell C2, it would recognise that the same thing was to happen and would add cells A2 and B2 (=A2+B2). All the formula has done is moved down one row: it is tracking the relative position of the other cell.

As shown in this example the formula is just moving the same formula down to the next row but making it relative to that row.

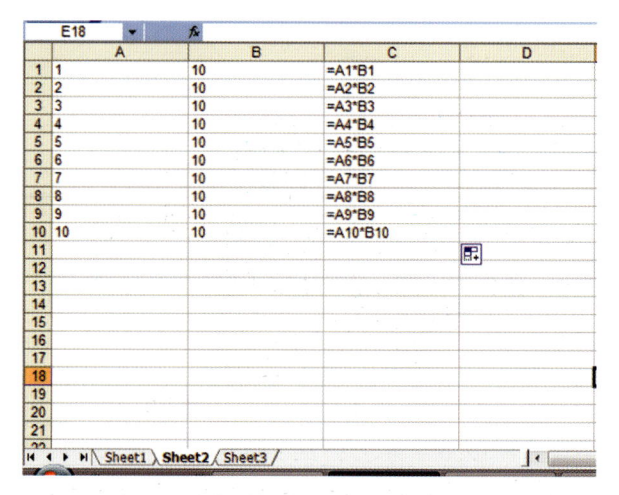

However, there are times when you may want to copy a formula but you don't want it to track the relative cell. This is called *Absolute Cell Referencing*. This is the opposite of *Relative Cell Referencing* where you want to track the relative position of the cell.

The spreadsheet below will help you understand. This spreadsheet works out how much in membership fees is owed by members of a fictitious football fan club. We want to multiply the number of weeks in cell C5 by the cost of membership in cell G4. Then copy the formula down. Set up the spreadsheet below and try this out.

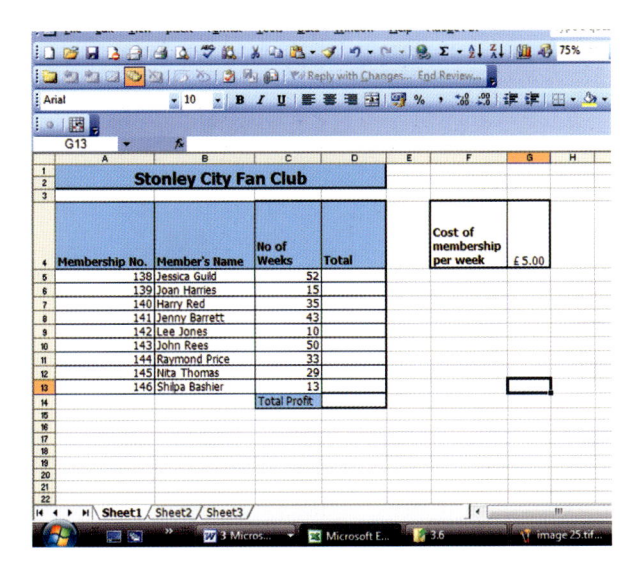

Notice that when you copy the formula, blanks will appear in cells D6 to D13. Let's have a look at the formulae to see why.

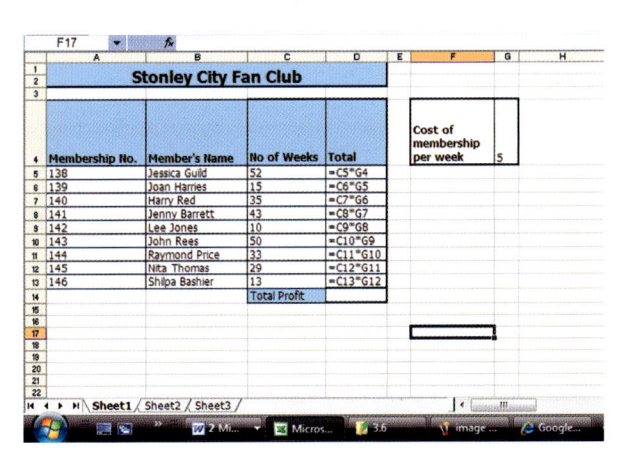

What's happened here is in cell D6 it has tracked the relative cell. It has multiplied cell C6 by G5. It has automatically guessed that we would want to multiply the next cell, not go back to G4 every time. However, we did not want this to happen, we wanted to multiply all the cells by G4 every time. But we need to tell the computer this is what we want to happen. We can do this using Absolute Cell Referencing. To do this all you need to do is make a slight change to your formula in cell D5. In order to tell the computer to use Absolute Cell Referencing put dollar signs around the letter of the cell you want it to keep using, e.g. = C5 * G4. Then when the formula is copied it will automatically stick to the same cell each time. Instead of typing the dollar sign a shortcut can be used; if you highlight G4 in the formula bar and press F4 on the keyboard, it will put the dollar signs in automatically.

Quick task

Recreate the fan club spreadsheet and use Absolute Cell Referencing to copy your formula. Also use a suitable formula to work out the total profit. Print your formulae making sure you can see the whole formula for each cell. You may need to put your page into landscape. (*File*, *Page Set-up*, *Landscape*)

Delete/insert data

You may be asked to insert or delete data in a spreadsheet. This is quite simple to do. Simply right click with the mouse on the row letter that is to be deleted and select *delete* from the options. To insert a row, again right click on the mouse and select *insert*: the new row always appears above the row selected.

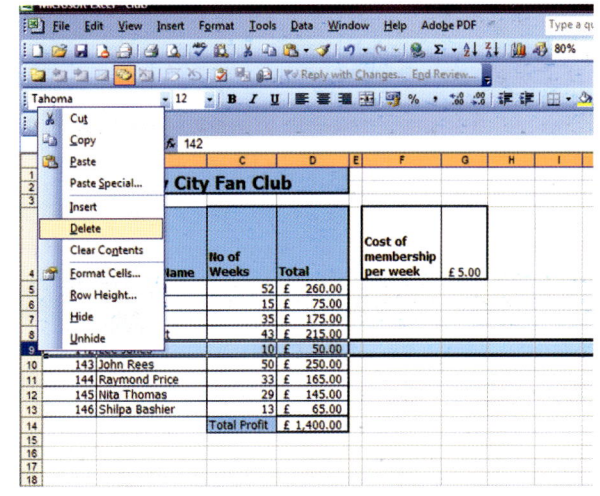

Other functions

Other types of functions that may be required are Average, Max and Min. Working out the Average can be done easily in a spreadsheet with one of its functions. In the example below is a list of test results for pupils in a class. To work out the average, click where the answer is to go (D12), then click on *Autosum* as in a previous example, but this time click on the black arrow and choose *Average* and press *enter*.

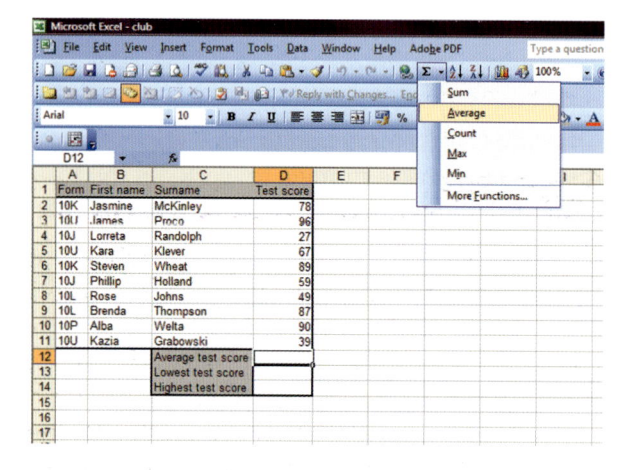

The formula it would return is =Average(D2:D11). For the highest score use Max and the lowest score use Min. Make sure, when working out the Max and the Min only cells D2:D11 are included in the formula.

Quick task

Try this spreadsheet out and print your functions.

Graphs and charts

Sometimes it's better to display numerical information in a graph or a chart: it is easier to spot trends and differences in this visual form. Graphs and charts can easily be created in spreadsheet software. We will be using the test results spreadsheet from the previous page.

Highlight the information you want to be included in your chart: for this chart we will just have surname and test scores. Do not include the headings, only the data we want to be included in the chart.

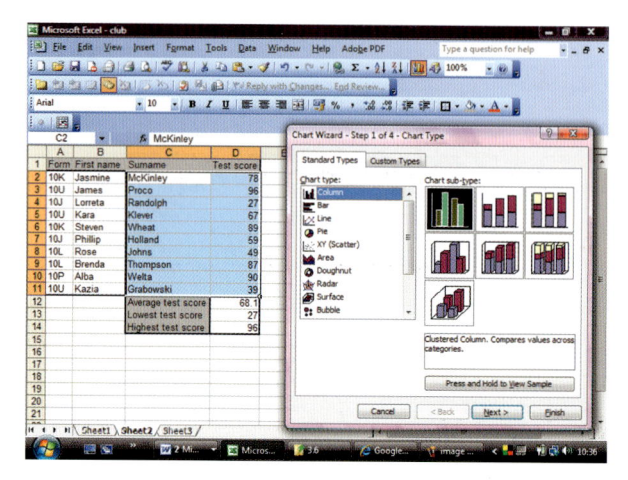

Then select the type of chart you want and click *next*. The next screen shows what the chart will look like. Click *next* again. A sensible chart title must be added, a category for the X axis, that is the one at the bottom and a value for your Y axis, that is the axis going up.

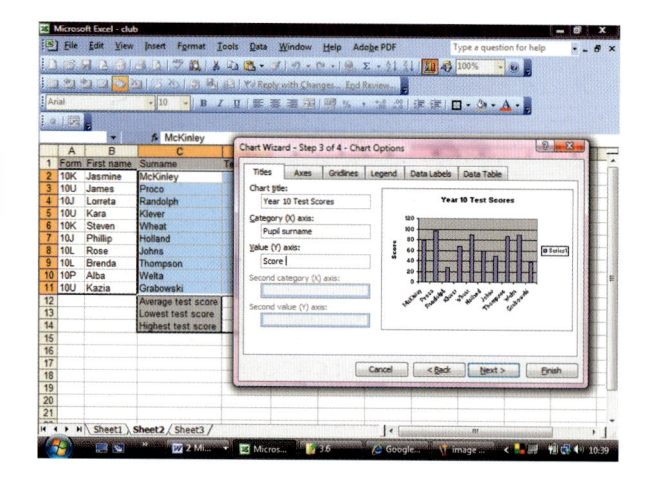

Click *next* and *finish* and the chart will appear with titles. Now try creating this chart for yourself.

Analysing numerical information using a spreadsheet   151

Tips

To delete the series, which is not needed when showing only one set of data, click on it and press delete on your keyboard. Also, it is possible to right click on the text in the chart and go to *Format* for options to make changes to the text.

More graphs and charts

Usually when asked to create a graph or chart the data you may want to include in the spreadsheet is not next to each other: this makes things a bit more difficult. We are going to go back to our fan club spreadsheet from the previous example to illustrate this.

We want to make a chart to include the member's name and how much membership they have paid. However, the information is not next to each other as it was in the test score spreadsheet example. This is more common when creating graphs and charts. To include information in your chart that is in separate parts of the spreadsheet, highlight the first section you would like to include: this will normally be the information that will be on the X axis like members' names (B5 to B13 in this example). Remember, do not include the title *Member's Name*. Then hold down *control* (CTRL) on your keyboard and don't let go. Then highlight the second part of the data to go into your chart: in this example it is the totals (D5 to D13). Now let go of the control key: notice that the data that you want to include in your graph is highlighted as shown in the diagram.

Then create your chart exactly as in the previous example.

Sorting

Another function available in a spreadsheet is *Sort*. Numbers and words can easily be sorted into numerical or alphabetical order. To do this you must click on the column you would like to sort, then click on the *Sort* icon on the main toolbar. Either *Sort Ascending*, this means starting at the lowest to the highest whether in numbers or letters, or *Sort Descending*, which does the opposite.

Benefits and drawbacks of spreadsheet software

Benefits:

- It allows you to perform calculations quickly.
- Hundreds of functions and formulae are available.
- Lots of short cuts are available like copying formulae.
- It allows you to create graphs and charts.
- It helps businesses create professional-looking documents.

Drawbacks:

- It can be quite difficult to use.
- There are lots of functions and formulae to remember.
- Training will be required to use the software to its full extent.
- Training can be expensive and take a long time.
- It is easy to make mistakes.

Consider what type of occupations use spreadsheets. Think about what sort of things they may use spreadsheets for.

Tasks

Task A

You are the assistant finance manager of a large chain of gyms. You were asked to arrange a training event for all Gym Managers held in London. All Gym Managers were allowed to claim expenses for the training event. They were allowed to claim for travel costs, food and overnight accommodation. You need to work out each person's expenses so you can give the money back.

1 Set up the spreadsheet as shown below.

A	B	C	D	E	F	G	H	I
Name	Start place	End place	Total mileage	Total cost of mileage	Hotel	Food	Total expense	Amount per mile
Corey Walton	Swansea	London	372		£130.00	£8.00		£0.30
Michael Cartwright	Coventry	London	190		£128.00	£53.00		
Ethan Gordon	Birmingham	London	232		£99.00	£48.00		
Amelia Clements	Wrexham	London	364		£110.00	£28.00		
Kieran Watson	Portsmouth	London	150		£162.00	£33.00		
Gabriel Kay	Glasgow	London	794		£132.00	£47.00		
Kai Bull	Manchester	London	395		£110.00	£75.00		
Maddison Hussain	Leeds	London	386		£182.00	£45.00		

Analysing numerical information using a spreadsheet 153

Note: Do not type in the pound signs where the cells are currency; type in the amount then convert the cells into currency by clicking Format *on the main toolbar, selecting* Cells *and then clicking* Currency. *Do this to all cells that will contain a currency value.*

2 Format your spreadsheet to improve the appearance.
3 Work out the total cost of mileage in cells E2 to E9. You will need to use Absolute Cell Referencing here.
4 Now work out the total expense for each person.
5 There has been a mistake with Gabriel Kay's hotel bill. It came to £153, not £132, and Amelia Clements' food bill was £23.00, not £28.00. Change the cells accordingly.
6 Print your formulae ensuring you can see all the information. Print onto a landscape page.
7 Create a column chart showing the total expenses for each person. Make sure you have sensible labels for your chart. Print your chart.

Extension Activities

a Use an appropriate formula to calculate the average total expenses per person.
b Use an appropriate formula to find out the highest mileage travelled.
c Use an appropriate formula to find out the lowest food bill of all the managers.
d Sort your total expenses into ascending order.
e Print your formulae ensuring you can see all the information. Print onto a landscape page.

Task B

Write a few paragraphs using word processing software to explain the benefits and drawbacks to your company of using spreadsheet software to calculate expenses.

Topic 3.7

Storing and managing customer and product records using a database

Aims

By the end of this topic you should be able to:
- **describe what a database is**
- **explain the various functions of a database**
- **create a database to perform a variety of tasks.**

A database is a collection of data stored in a structured way. A database is structured into fields and records. Fields are the headings in a database; for example, if a teacher had a database of all the pupils in a class, the types of fields in the database could be First Name, Last Name, Date of Birth, Form Group, Target Level etc. A record in a database is all the information about one person or thing. So in the database of all the pupils in a teacher's class, all the information about one pupil would be a record.

First name	Last name	DoB	Form Group	Target level
Reece	Saunders	19.09.88	7C	4
Sofia	Gray	01.07.88	7Y	5
Brandon	Wilkins	03.10.88	7Y	5
Elizabeth	Lee	17.01.88	7H	4
Courtney	Shaw	11.03.88	7L	5

A database can be created about any topic: at home you may create a database of all your friends' and family's details. In a business, they may store customer, product and staff details in databases. Once the database is set up there are many functions available to perform a variety of tasks. We are going to create a database for an estate agent, which holds the details of houses. This will then help us to learn about some of the functions available to us. Start a new blank database and call it 'estate agent'. Create a table in the *Design View* and then enter the following Field Names and Data Types.

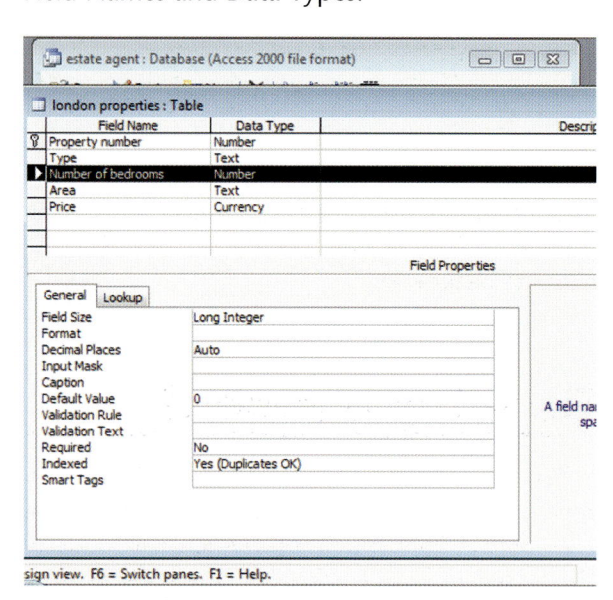

Field Name	Data Type
Property number	Number
Type	Text
Number of bedrooms	Number
Area	Text
Price	Currency

Save your work and enter the following records in the *Data Sheet View*.

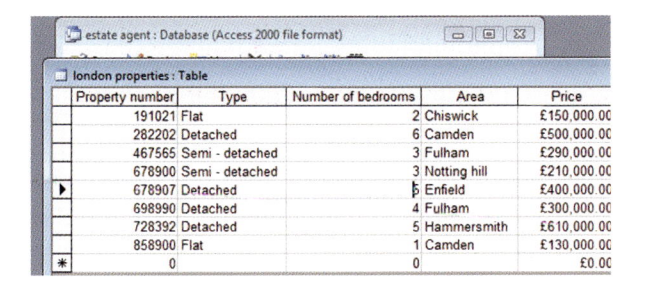

Storing and managing customer and product records using a database | **155**

> Think about the types of organisation that would use database software. What sort of information would they hold? What sort of fields would they have?

Editing data

When asked to edit data in a database, it basically means something must be changed in the database. For example, there might be a mistake in the database that needs editing.

Tasks

Task 1

The estate agent made a mistake: property number 191021 is £170,000.00, not £150,000.00. Edit the database.

Deleting a record

When asked to delete a record in a database it means it is no longer needed. To do this, right click on the grey square on the left-hand side of the record that needs deleting, then select *delete record*.

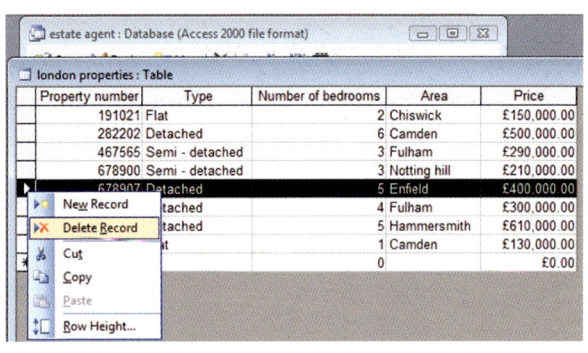

Tasks

Task 2

Property 282202 has been sold; delete the record.

Sorting

Sorting a database allows data to be sorted into numerical or alphabetical order. There are two options available here: fields can either be sorted into ascending or descending order. Ascending order is the earliest first, so either A to Z on records with text inside them or starting at the lowest number to the highest number in records that contain numerical data. Descending is the complete opposite, either highest number to lowest number or Z to A with text records. To sort a field just click on the field to be sorted and then click one of the two *sort* buttons. These can be found on the main toolbar as shown below.

Tasks

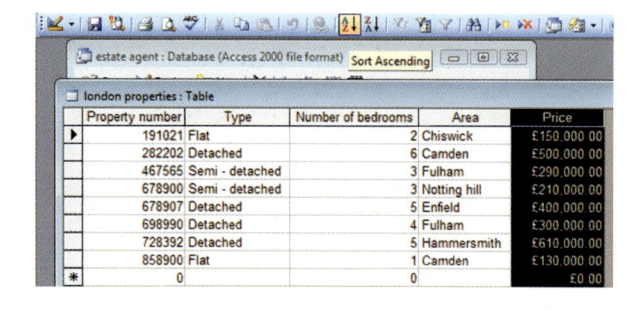

Task 3

Sort the field Price into descending order. The most expensive property should appear at the top.

Unique record identifier

Let's take another look at the estate agent's database. The first field 'Property number' is a very important field. Consider the database without the 'Property number' field: could it be possible that in a large estate agent's database that some of the data in the records could be the same? Look at the first record: could it be possible that there is more than one two-bedroom flat for sale in Chiswick priced at £150,000.00? The answer is yes. This is why we need to have a Unique Record Identifier: it is also called the *Key Field* and in Microsoft Access software it is called the *Primary Key*. We will call it the *Key Field*. It is basically a unique number that every record will have so that it is different from the rest. Another example could be a staff database; if a business had a database of its entire staff, could it be possible that two people have the same name? The answer is yes, of course it could be possible, so they will have a Key Field, with a unique number for every record: it may be called staff number or employee number.

It is usually necessary to tell the software which field is to be the Key Field when creating a database in the *Design View*. This can be done by right clicking on the field that is to be the Key Field and selecting *Primary Key*. A key appears to the left of the field name. Then when you are in the *Data Sheet View* where data is entered, you cannot enter the same number twice. Remember the Key Field has to be a unique number.

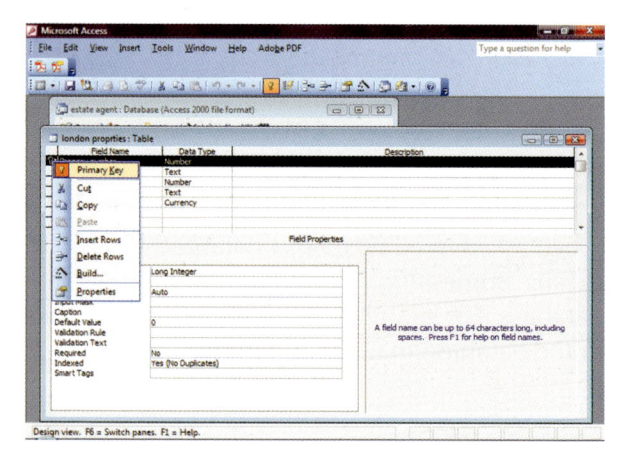

Why not try it out? See what happens if you try and put the same number in twice.

Creating queries to search for specific data

A query is when a database is searched to find things that match certain criteria. This can easily be done in a database and is a very useful tool, especially in organisations that have databases which hold thousands of records. To set up a query click *Queries* in the database window and select *create query* in the *Design View*. Then select *add* and *close* and it will take you to the screen to

Storing and managing customer and product records using a database

create your query. The screen below is where you will select your field and enter your criteria.

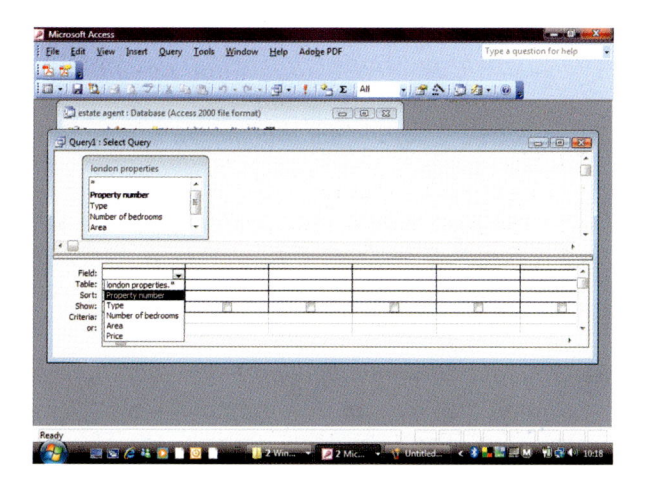

To select the field you want to do a query on, click the drop-down menu and select the field; for this example, we will select *Area*. Then in the section called *Criteria*, enter the words that you want to search for. For this example we want to find all the properties in the Fulham area.

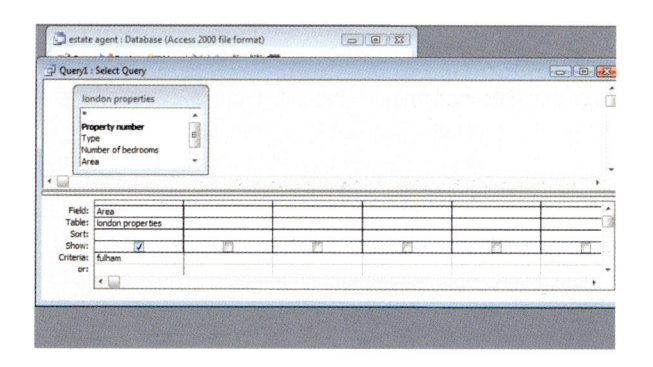

To run the query, click *Query* on the main toolbar and select *run*.

It should return two properties in Fulham, if everything has been entered and spelt correctly.

Then save the query with a sensible name. If you wanted to find the property numbers of the houses in Fulham, when creating the query and selecting fields select both 'Property number' and 'Area' as shown below.

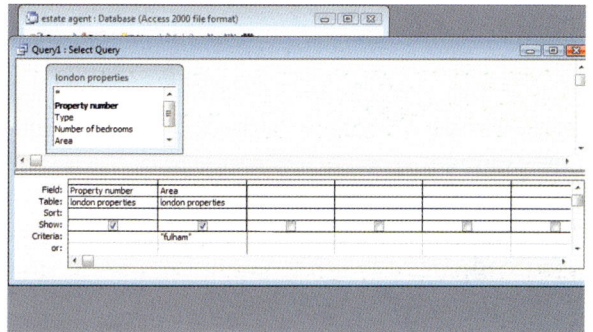

Run the query as you would normally. You can search on as many fields as you want with as many criteria as you want.

Tasks

Task 4

Do a query to find the property numbers of all the properties in Enfield in the estate agent's database.

More queries

You can search for numbers in a database, so for example you could search for all the properties with two bedrooms.

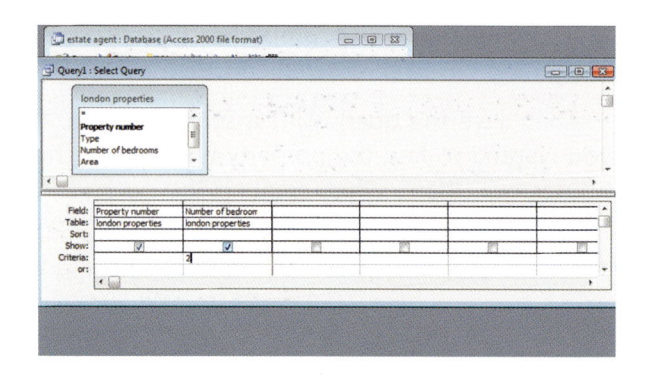

It is also possible to do queries for numbers over a certain amount or under a certain amount. For example, if a person came into the estate agents and wanted to find a property under £120,000.00, in the criteria section use the less-than sign <. You may have used this sign in your maths class. The sign for greater than is >; these signs can be found on your keyboard. To find all the properties that are £120,000.00 and over, you want to include the properties that are £120,000.00 then you must use the equal sign as well, e.g. >=120000. Please note, do not use the pound sign, even if searching on a field that contains currency. Also do not use commas. Using these signs will prevent the query from working.

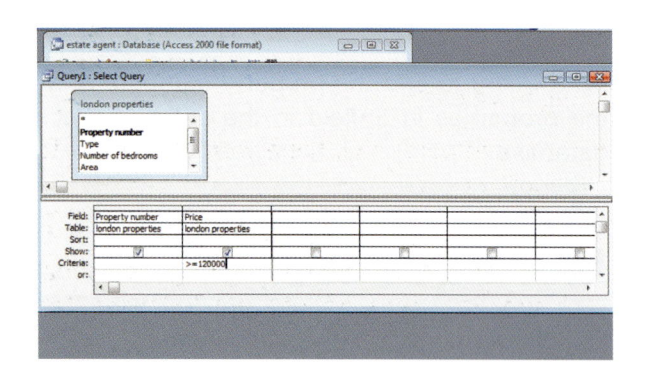

Tasks

Do a query to find all the properties worth over £120,000.00

Tasks

Try out the following queries:

1. Do a query to find all the property numbers of the flats.
2. A customer would like to know if you have any semi-detached properties in Fulham; you will need to find the property numbers as well. Do a query to find this out.
3. A customer wants a property for £400,000.00 or over and it must be detached. Do a query to find the property numbers of the properties that fit his specification.

Creating reports from queries

Once you have completed a query, you may want to print the results. There are a few choices here. You could just print in the normal view, which is fine but does not look very professional. A database can be printed professionally as a report: this is a much better way of presenting a query, especially if it is to be viewed by someone else. To do this, go back to the database window and select *Report*. Select *create report* using wizard. Select the query that you wish to make a report from in the drop down list – the choice is yours – then click the double arrows *(>>)* to send all the fields that you want to use to the next screen. If you want to leave fields out of your report you can send them across individually using the single arrow *(>)*.

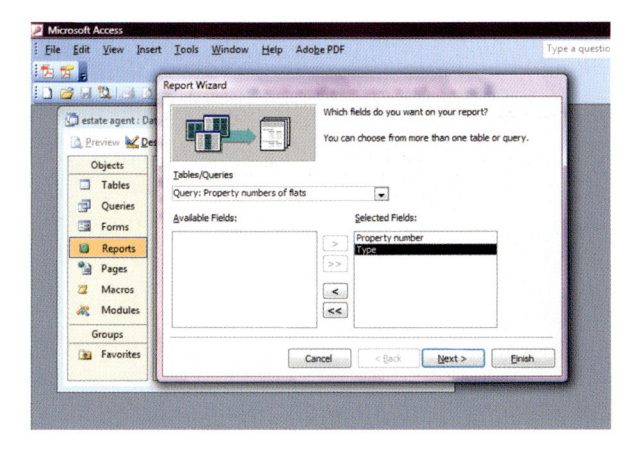

Storing and managing customer and product records using a database 159

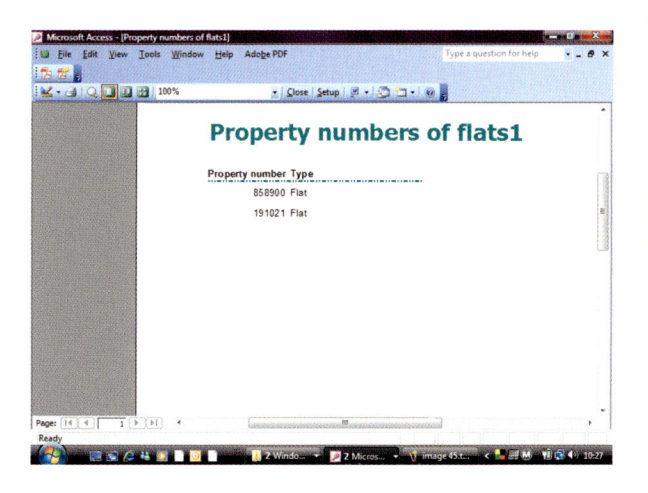

The advantages and disadvantages of database software

Database software is very useful. Its functions include sorting, queries and reports. There are benefits and drawbacks of database software.

Benefits:

- You can save time finding information compared to a paper database.
- You can sort information into order.
- You can search for information that meets a certain criteria quickly and easily.
- You can produce professional-looking reports.
- You can select data types such as text or currency; this will help prevent mistakes.

Drawbacks:

- Equipment and software can be expensive to buy.
- Training will be required to use the software to its full extent: this training can be expensive for organisations.
- If the computers fail, there won't be access to important data.
- There may be issues with security: it is important that when storing personal information, organisations are following the Data Protection Act.

Mail-merge

The mail-merge facility allows two pieces of software to be brought together. It is possible to link the data in a database to a word-processing document. So, for example, if a business has all the details of its customers in a database and wanted to send a similar letter to all of them, this

The next screen wants you to choose any grouping levels. For this type of small report and the type you would be expected to do for this subject, there is no need to change anything here: just click *next*. The next screen allows any sorting of fields in the query: we will sort 'Property number' into ascending order. However, it is not important to do this unless you are asked to in an exam.

The next screen asks you to choose how you would like to lay out your report: either choose *Tabular* or *Columnar*, *Landscape* or *Portrait*. Choose the option that best suits the amount of data in your query. The next stage allows you to choose a style of report. Then click *finish* and the report is ready for printing; it will look similar to the report shown below. Notice that the name of your query will appear as the heading: that is why it is important that you name your query with a suitable name. In business, reports will be much larger and contain a lot more information.

could be done easily using both pieces of software. Also, the mail-merge facility allows organisations to give a personal touch to its letters: instead of writing *Dear Sir/Madam*, with the mail-merge facility, it is possible to personalise a letter by writing name, address and other details into the letter. An example will make this clearer.

Firstly, it is necessary to have a database to work with. The database will contain the customers' details of the estate agent in the previous example. Create the following database as shown earlier. This is the structure of the fields:

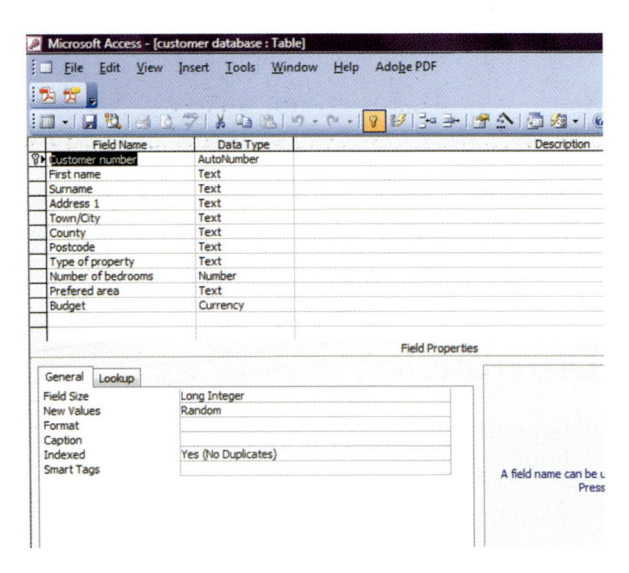

Once the database is set up, enter sensible, fictitious data into the database in the *Data Sheet View*. Enter about five records. To prepare the letter head, open a Word document and enter the details of the estate agent as shown below. Remember to use the fully blocked style with open punctuation for the business letter.

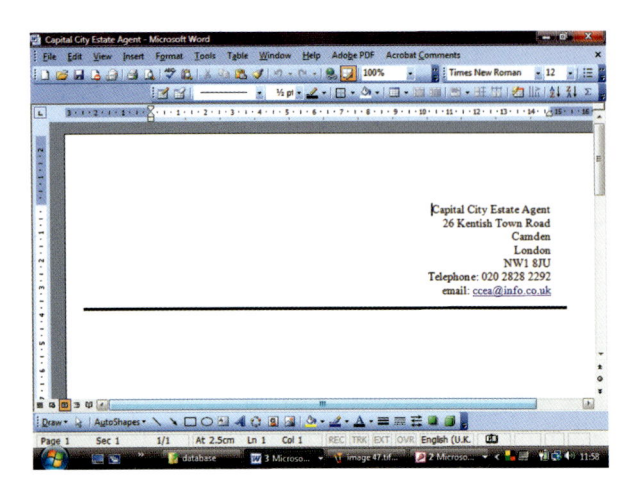

Save the letter head with a sensible name in an appropriate place. Go back to the database in the *Data Sheet View*; go to *Tools* on the main toolbar; select *Office Links*; and merge it with MS Word.

The following window will appear. There are two options: if the letter head has been created already, which it has, select the first option; if not, for future reference select the second. Both will link to a Word document, but the first one will give the option to find a file that has previously been saved, like the letter head.

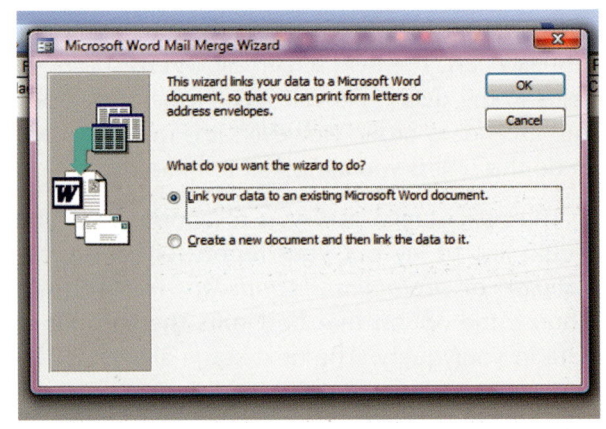

The two documents are now linked. The letter now needs to be set up in the *Template View* before the details in the database and the Word document are merged together.

Quick thought

Why is it better for organisations to personalise letters?

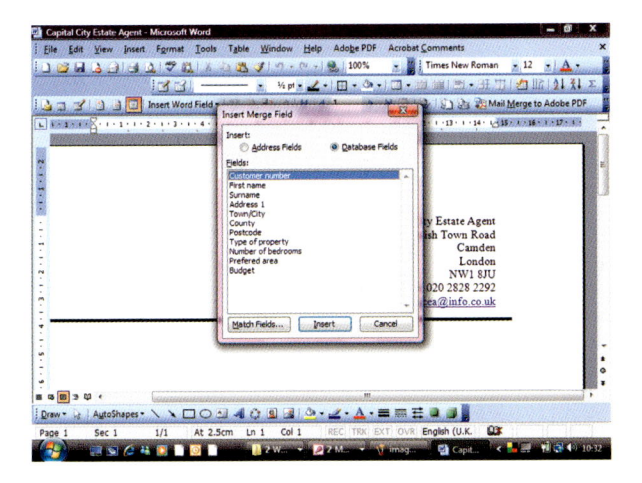

Storing and managing customer and product records using a database

Select the icon shown above called *Insert Merge Fields*: the fields in the database then appear in a window as shown. To select the required fields: click on them; click the *insert* button and click *close*; then repeat the process until the document looks as shown below.

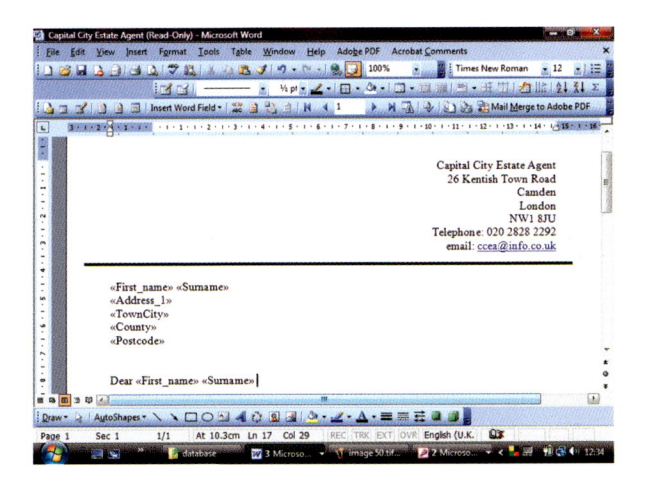

When the letter has been written, to merge the two documents together, click on the icon called *Merge to New Document* on the mail-merge toolbar, as shown below.

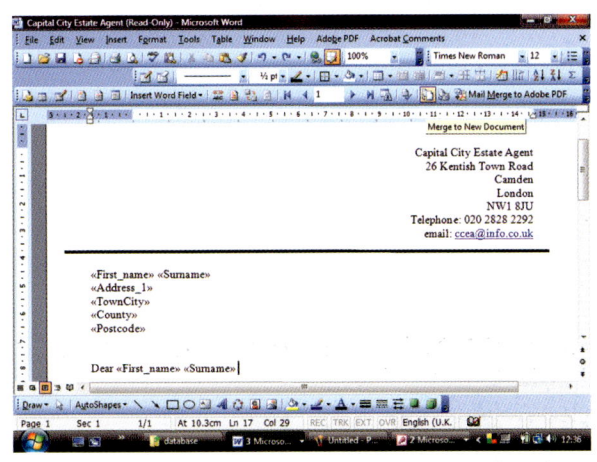

Tasks

1. Complete the letter on the previous page by telling the customer of the estate agent that Capital City Estate Agents will be changing offices to a larger location. The new address will be 77 Parkway, Camden, London NW1 7UO; the phone number and email will remain the same. Tell the customers that there will be an open evening for all buyers and sellers to view the new premises on Monday 13 August at 7.00 pm; all are welcome.

   Close the letter with the correct complimentary close. Print the letter as a standard document and print one copy of the merged letter.

2. Sort the customer database into alphabetical order by customer surname, and print it.

3. Do a query to find the full names and customer numbers of all the customers with a budget of over £150,000.00. Save the query with a sensible name.

4. Create a report to display the query created in the previous task. Print the completed report.

Extension

Design some complex queries; try them out and then make them into reports.

Topic 3.8

Organising diaries and meetings using diary management software

Aims

By the end of this topic you should be able to:
- describe what diary management software is
- explain the features of diary management software
- analyse the advantages and disadvantages of diary management software.

In an organisation it is very important that people's time is well-planned and not wasted, or the business will not be well organised. Diary management software is often used by organisations to help staff do this. Diary management software works as a personal organiser on a computer. Before computers, people would use a diary or a personal organiser to write down appointments and events; nowadays staff often use diary management software to help them plan tasks. The software also allows emails and communications to be received. Contact lists and reminders can also be created. This software is very useful to the business to allow staff to plan their time and communicate effectively.

Calendars

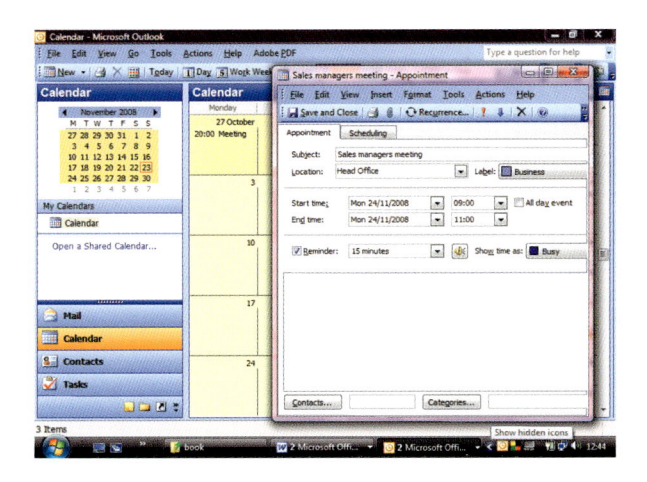

A commonly-used diary management program is Microsoft Outlook ®: one of the features of this software is the calendar. The image below shows how appointments and events are set up: appointments can be set up on certain days; timescales can be added. Reminders can also be set so appointments and events are not missed. Also it is possible to publish a calendar so work colleagues are able to see everyone else's schedule.

Arranging meetings using diary management software

Meetings can easily be arranged with groups of people using the software: the time and date of the meeting can be entered into the appointment manager feature; this can then be sent to all the people who are invited to the meeting. This will automatically update in their calendar and it can be set up so they get a reminder about the meeting. People can respond 'yes' or 'no' to attending a meeting. Agendas can also be sent as attachments.

Quick thought

What sort of events would people in a business enter into a calendar in diary management software?

Tasks and 'to do' lists

Lists of tasks and activities with deadlines can be entered into the software. This is a sort of detailed 'to do' list. This allows staff to keep track of the tasks that they have been set, to look at progress made and to keep to important deadlines.

Email

Diary management software can be used to collect and send emails. By connecting the software to the email server it is possible to collect and send emails from accounts. This will then synchronise with the email server. So if a person had an email account in work and a Hotmail account for personal use, for example, they could set it up so all the emails from the work account and their Hotmail account could be received in the diary management software. There would be no need to go onto the internet and log onto an email service provider.

Managing contacts

Contact lists can also be set up with all the details of the contacts: this is basically a sophisticated address book. Various details can be added such as email addresses, phone numbers etc. It is also possible to add a picture of the person to the contacts lists and details of their business and position. Contact details can be easily forwarded to other people.

Benefits:

- Staff time can be planned efficiently.
- Helps to stop meetings and appointments clashing.
- It is possible to synchronise with mobile technology such as a PDA.
- Allows managers to easily track workers' schedules.
- Allows teams to easily communicate.

Drawbacks:

- Over-reliance on computers: if the computers fail, there isn't a record of staffs' schedules.
- Can be quite tricky to use: staff may require expensive training.
- The software has to be bought and installed on every PC, which has a cost.
- May lead to lack of face-to-face communication.
- Time could be wasted emailing and planning appointments rather than getting on with the task.

Tasks

1. A large charity, whose aim is to raise money to stop cruelty to animals, has asked you to advise them on whether to buy diary management software for the organisation. At the moment fundraisers often find themselves double-booked on meetings and communication is a problem. However, the organisation is a charity, therefore spending this money on installing the software and training staff has to be justified. Write a report to the managing director of the charity, Angela Tumbridge, to advise her on what you think she should do.

Topic 3.9

Managing projects using project management software

Aims

By the end of this topic you should be able to:
- describe what project management software is
- explain the features of project management software
- analyse the advantages and disadvantages of project management software.

There are many different types of project management software available: the ability to use this software is not required for this subject. However, there is a need to understand the software and to answer questions about it.

What is a project?

A project is basically any task that is done to achieve a particular aim. People undertake projects all the time, e.g. planning a holiday, organising an event. In organisations people and teams of people are often given projects to complete: how this is organised is very important to the success of a project. If things are not organised well then the aim may not be achieved.

Examples of projects

In organisations the type of projects that might take place are:

- organising a training event
- organising the introduction of new software
- launching a new product.

Quick thought

What other type of projects might take place in a business?

These projects don't just happen; new products and training events don't just appear; massive amounts of time and planning go into these types of projects. Often many people are involved: people are very often organised into teams. All the people in the team will have the same aim and may be given individual tasks to help achieve the aim.

Project management software

Teams of people are often given projects to complete. These projects can be quite big and require a lot of planning. Many people are often involved in these tasks. All this needs to be organised and a way of doing this is using project management software which helps everyone plan the different stages of the project. Each person can be assigned tasks using the software and the project and tasks can be given timescales and deadlines. This allows people to monitor their progress. It also allows managers to monitor the progress of people in their teams. It is possible to produce a Gannt chart using project management software. This allows a whole project to be broken up into tasks or activities. It allows people to be assigned tasks and allows timescales to be worked out.

Date/tasks	Person	01/10/08	08/10/08	15/10/08	22/10/08	29/10/08	05/11/08	12/11/08	19/11/08	26/11/08	02/12/08	09/12/08	16/12/08
Organise the venue	HJ	■	■										
Organise overnight accommodation	UN		■	■									
Organise transport and parking	KI				■	■							
Organise IT equipment	FT					■	■						
Organise guest speaker	BY						■	■					
Organise stationery and supplies	MY							■					
Organise lunch	RT									■			
Organising finances	OP	■	■	■	■	■	■	■	■	■	■	■	■
Organising finances	NR	■	■	■	■	■	■	■	■	■	■	■	■

Example of a Gannt chart

The above Gannt chart is for the organisation of a training event. The first column shows the task names and is followed by the initials of the person in charge of that task. The coloured areas show the timescales assigned to each of the tasks. Some tasks in the project take longer than others like organising finance, for instance, that is ongoing throughout the project, whereas organising stationery and supplies only takes up to one week. People may work on a few different projects at any one time.

Tracking costs using project management software

Project management software also allows the team to work to a budget: it can track any expenditure and if costs are over-running it becomes apparent. The main aim of project management software is that tasks are run efficiently and deadlines are met. If there are any potential delays they can be picked up in the software and methods can be put in place to rectify them.

Benefits and drawbacks of project management software

Benefits:

- Tasks can be organised into manageable tasks.
- Progress is easily monitored, which keeps everyone involved in the task.
- Highlights any potential problems before they happen, such as timescales not being met.
- Costs can easily be tracked and costs are kept within a budget.

Drawbacks:

- Software can be expensive.
- Staff may require expensive training to use the software.
- Software can be complicated to use and may need expensive experts to run it.
- Time can be wasted focusing on using the software rather than completing the project.

Tasks

1 List four features of project management software.

2 State two possible uses for project management software.

3 Describe the benefits and drawbacks of using project management software

4 Explain the impact that project management software could have on a business.

Topic 3.10

Sharing information on the web using blogs and wikis

Aims

By the end of this topic you should be able to:
- describe what blogs and wikis are
- explain the features of blogs and wikis
- be able to evaluate the advantages and disadvantages of blogs and wikis.

Blogs

The word blog is short for 'web log'. Blogs are a type of website found on the internet which allow people or businesses to provide comments or articles on a particular subject. There are a few types of blog available including personal blogs and business blogs. A personal blog allows anyone to write a commentary about any topic they wish. People can then make comments about the stories or articles on the blog. Anyone can create a blog about any topic.

How do businesses use blogs?

Businesses have started using blogs as a marketing or advertising tool or a way of communicating with their customers. For example, as part of a business's website, the business could add a blog where they could post items about new products or services or share news about the business. People could then make comments about the posts on the blog. Comments are posted in reverse chronological order, so the most recent comment made will be at the top of the screen.

It is hoped that through sharing information on a blog people will find out about a business's products and services and possibly buy them. Discussions may start about the posts on the blog: this will allow customers to find out everything they want to know about the business. For example an online mail order company that sells fashion clothes may have a blog. They may post items about new styles or celebrity fashion: readers can then comment on the posts. Have a look at the following link to a company that does just that: http://asostoday.asos.com/.

Quick task

Have a look at some of the posts and comments on the website. What sort of impact do you think this facility has on the business?

It is possible to allow customers to subscribe to a blog. They will then receive an email to alert them every time there is a new post on the blog: this will allow customers to find out about new products or services. The business hopes that through this more people will find out about and buy their products or services.

Blogs are an excellent form of communication with a business's customers. Through a blog businesses can find out what their customers really think of their products and services. People are more honest on a blog because they can be anonymous. However, if the business can screen comments and decides not to post them, the public may not find negative comments on a blog. Essentially the business can control the comments made.

A blog, like a website, allows businesses to reach a wider geographical market, so instead of just being able to tell people in their town about their products and services, the whole world is able to visit their blog and find out information.

Benefits:

- Can share information easily with their customers.
- Businesses can find out what their customers really want.
- Businesses can advertise to a wide geographical area.
- Blogs are relatively cheap to run.

Drawbacks:

- Can take a lot of time to constantly update.
- Customers can leave negative comments.
- An expert is needed to set up a blog, which can be expensive.
- The business or blogger can control the content of the blog.

Wikis

Wikis are another type of website that allow the public to add to or change its content. They can be a bit like an encyclopaedia on the internet, with information about almost any topic you can think of. However, the difference is anyone can add to or edit its contents and make comments. One of the major criticisms of this type of wiki is that they are not always accurate as anyone can write on them.

How do businesses use wikis?

Wikis are used by businesses on their intranets. An intranet is like an internal website that can only be accessed from within the business. The intranet will have information on it relating to the business, such as policies and procedures. Businesses have started creating wikis that staff can add content to about various topics to do with the business: this is a form of communication where work colleagues can trade information.

One of the wiki's main uses in business is teamwork on a project. For example, if a team of people were asked to work together on a document like a report, for example, they could create this as a wiki page: each person would be assigned a section to work on, then all the team could add to and edit the document. So instead of using email and sending attachments resulting in lots of different versions of the same piece of work, you get a live working document, where changes can be made and comments can be added. This is an excellent way to work as a team and create discussions.

Benefits:

- Saves a business time when creating a project as a team.
- Quick method of trading information with work colleagues.
- Lots of people can work on one document.
- Managers can keep a close eye on the progress of projects.

Drawbacks:

- People can edit other people's work.
- May cause friction in a workplace if people edit each other's work.
- Can be difficult to control its content.
- Comments cannot be controlled as with a blog.

Tasks

1 Explain what is meant by the term 'blog'.

2 Explain what is meant by the term 'wiki'.

3 Explain the difference between a blog and a wiki.

4 A business has created a blog to inform customers about new products. Customers are able to leave comments on the blog site in response to articles. Explain the benefits and drawbacks to the business of using a blog for this purpose.

5 A business has asked a team of four employees to create the text for a new publicity brochure. The business has decided to use a wiki to create the text. Assess the benefits and drawbacks to the business of using a wiki for this purpose.

Topic 3.11

Preparing for the examination

This unit of the qualification is worth 25% of the overall grade. Assessment of this unit will take the form of a practical exam: the exam will last one hour and will assess your work produced on the computer. Your work will then be sent off to an external examiner to mark. You will be told to print various pieces of evidence throughout the exam: you must make sure your details are on each printout or they cannot be accepted. Your teacher will give you further instructions. The exam paper will also explain exactly what information is to be included. The exam will consist of two tasks that you have to complete during the hour examination. Each task will be broken up into a number of smaller tasks.

To prepare for the exam you should become familiar with the following software:

- spreadsheets
- databases
- word processing software
- desk top publishing software
- web design software
- graphics software.

You should also be able to discuss the above software and its features in detail. Other types of software you should be able to discuss are project management software, diary management software and the others discussed in this book. To prepare for the practical exam it is a good idea to work your way through the tasks in this unit. This and the support of your teacher should give you the skills needed for the exam. In the next section you will find some exam-style questions. To complete these, set up the following spreadsheet and save it.

Staff ID number	Staff Name	Job Title	Hours worked	Hourly Rate	Weekly Pay	Deduction	Take home pay
102030	N Thomas	Manager		£10.00			
102920	T Morgan	Assistant manager		£8.00			
192020	O Williams	Supervisor		£7.00			
189303	C Simpson	Salesperson		£6.00			
183932	D Jones	Cleaner		£5.80			

Exam-style questions

You are the assistant manager of a small furniture shop. You want to start using spreadsheet software to calculate staff wages. Complete the following tasks based on the spreadsheet you have set up.

Tasks

Task 1

a You need to enter the hours each member of staff has worked this week. Enter the following data.

   N Thomas – 35

   T Morgan – 41

   O Williams – 42

   C Simpson – 34

   D Jones – 12   (5 marks)

b O Williams has been given a pay rise: her new pay is £7.50 per hour. Edit in the spreadsheet.
                                                                                                          (1 mark)

c A new salesperson has been employed. The person's name is Y Lewis; their staff ID number is 182928; they worked 21 hours last week. They will also be paid £7.50 per hour. Insert a row underneath O Williams and enter their data.   (6 marks)

d Create a formula to calculate the weekly pay of N Thomas. Then fill the formula down to calculate the other staff members' weekly pay.   (2 marks)

e Staff have to pay deductions, such as income tax and National Insurance etc., out of their weekly pay: this figure is 26% of their weekly pay. Create a formula in cell G2 to work out 26% of N Thomas' pay. Then replicate the formula down to work out the other members of staff.
                                                                                                          (2 marks)

f Now work out the take-home pay for each member of staff.   (2 marks)

g Print your spreadsheet in landscape in the *Formula View*.   (2 marks)

Task 2

a   The manager has told you he wants you to organise a full staff meeting.

The meeting is to be held in the manager's office at 5.00 pm Monday, 1 February 2010.

Write a Notice of Meeting and Agenda including the standard fixed items and the following information in the Agenda:

- January's sales
- February's promotions
- database software.

(12 marks)

b   The manager is considering purchasing database software to store all stock details. At the moment stock-lists are stored in a paper filing system and this system has its problems.

She would like you to create a presentation using presentation software to show in the meeting. The purpose of the presentation is to explain to her and staff what database software is as well as the features of database software. You must also explain the advantages and disadvantages of the software and explain the impact it could have on the business.

You will be expected to demonstrate some of the features of presentation software. You will also be expected to provide speaker notes with further information.

(18 marks)

Index

Abbreviations used:
ICT = information and communications technology

absolute cell referencing 148–9
access
   to information 34–6
   unauthorised 38, 51, 62, 74
access rights 76–7
accidents, at work 29–30
advertising 24, 32, 42
adware 74, 78
agenda 125–6
Amazon 80, 82–3
animations, in presentations 139
anti-virus software 78
applications software 61
archive storage, manual systems 47–8
autosum (∑) 147

back-up systems
   and copyright 37
   frequency 71–2
   procedures 71
   storage 66, 72–3
bankruptcy 10
barcodes 44–5, 64
benchmarking 17
blogs 167–8
blu-ray 69–70
body language 99
borders 133, 135
briefings 95
British Airways 12
broadband 80
brochures 97, 134–6
businesses
   de-layering 8
   e-commerce, benefits/drawbacks of 82
   ethics 42–3
   expansion 10
   external influences on 12–13

failure of 2, 10–11
functional areas 7
and law 27, 30, 33, 35–8, 45
location 11
new, reasons for starting 2
objectives 10–11
role in society 43
social responsibility 42–3
stakeholders of 105–6
structures 7–8
success, reasons for 11
types of 4–5

calendars 163–4
call centres 18, 100
cash flow 11
cathode ray tube (CRT) monitors 57
cells, in spreadsheets 146, 148–9
central processing units (CPU) 61
chain of command 8
charts 140, 150–1
cold-calling 100
colour, use in DTP 133, 135–6
columns 136
communication
   barriers to 108
   choice of method 91–2, 108
   defining 90–1
   devices for 101–4
   errors in 44
   external 91, 97–100, 167–8
   improving, procedures for 45
   internal 91–6
   poor 45, 107–8
   private/public communication 91
   verbal 95–6, 99–100
   written 93–4, 97–8, 167–8
compact discs (CD-ROM/CD-R/CD-RW) 69, 72
companies 5
Companies House 5
competition 11, 12

Index

competitiveness
  improving 24–5
  monitoring 21–2
computer-based systems
  benefits/drawbacks 50–1
  manual systems, compared with 51
  security 38, 51, 62, 74–9, 111
computer fraud 38
computer hardware
  computing devices 61–4
  input devices 52–5
  output devices 57–60
computer memory
  hard disks, internal/external 61–2, 66, 72
  portable flash drives/memory cards 67
Computer Misuse Act 1990 38
computer monitors 30, 56–7
computer security 38, 51, 62, 74–9, 111
computer software 61, 78
computers
  desktop computers 61–2
  electronic point of sale (EPOS) devices 64
  health and safety law on 30
  laptop computers 63–4
  software audits 38
  unauthorised access 38, 51, 62, 74
concept format keyboards 53
conference programmes 127
confidentiality 92, 94
consumer protection law 32–3, 45
contacts, managing 164
copyright 37–8
Copyright, Designs and Patents Act 1988 37–8
corporate social responsibility 42–3
costs
  of communication errors 45
  of ICT-based systems 110, 115
  managing 166
cropping graphics 129
cultural issues, and poor communication 107
customer satisfaction *see also* customer service
  as business objective 10–11
  importance of 14
  measuring, methods of 15–17
customer service 7
  defining 19
  importance of 25
  policies/standards 17–18
  poor, impact of 19–20, 108
  speed of response time 25
customers
  e-commerce, benefits/drawbacks of 81
  face-to-face meetings with 99
  poor communication with, impact of 108
  as stakeholders 105
  telephone communication with 99–100

data projectors 58
data protection 34–6
Data Protection Act 1998 34–6
databases
  benefits/drawbacks 159
  defining 154
  editing/deleting data 154–5
  mail-merge 159–61
  queries 156–8
  reports 158–9
  sorting data 155–6
  unique record identifiers 156
de-layering business structures 8
desk top publishing (DTP) software 132–6
  benefits/drawbacks 133–4
  creating brochures/newsletters 134–6
  features of 132–6
desktop computers 61–2
diary management software 163–4
digital cameras 45
directors 7–8, 105
discrimination 26
dismissal, of employees 27
documents for business, creating
  conference/training programmes 127
  using databases 154–61
  using desk top publishing (DTP) software 132–6
  using graphics software 129–31
  letters 97, 120–2
  meeting notices/agenda 125–6
  memorandum/memo 93, 123–4
  using presentation software 138–41
  using spreadsheets 146–52
  using web creation software 143–5
domain names 80
dot-matrix printers 59–60
DTP (desk top publishing software)
  benefits/drawbacks 133–4
  creating brochures/newsletters 134–6

Index

features of 132–6
DVDs (digital versatile discs) 69

e-commerce
   benefits/drawbacks 81–2
   defining 80
   equipment/systems necessary for 80–1
   payment systems 80, 82
e-mail 94, 98, 123
   and diary management software 163–4
   security precautions 75
   SPAM 74–5
editing graphics 129
electrical equipment, disposal of 40–1
electronic equipment, disposal of 40–1
electronic point of sale (EPOS) devices 64
employees
   and changes to ICT 115–16
   discipline and dismissal 27
   and health and safety law 29
   job roles/working practices 115–16
   pay and conditions 26–7
   poor communication with, impact of 108
   re-skilling 115
   recruitment 26
   redundancy 27, 116
   remote working 115–16
   as stakeholders 105
employers
   and employment law 26–7
   and health and safety law 29–30
employment law 26–7
encryption 78–9
End-of-Life Vehicles Regulations 2003 41
entrepreneurs 2–3
environmental protection 40–1
environmental sustainability, of ICT 111
equal pay 26
errors, in business communications 44–5
ethics, in business 42–3
extranets 94

facsimile (fax) 101
fileservers, network 62, 77
filing systems
   computer-based 50–1
   manual 47–8, 51
finance departments 7

firewalls 78
flash drives, portable 67
flat business structures 8
flyers 97
focus groups 15
fonts 133, 136
formulae, in spreadsheets 147–50
frames 133–4, 136
franchises 6
fraud 38
Freedom of Information Act 2000 36
fully blocked letter style 120–2

Gannt charts 165–6
goods 7
   bought by post/telephone/online 33
   consumer protection 32–3
Google Mail 72
government
   as stakeholder 106
   websites 143
graphics software 129–31
   benefits/drawbacks 130
graphs 140, 150–1
gross misconduct 27

hacking 38, 51, 62, 74
handheld computer devices 63–4
hard disks, internal/external 61–2, 66, 72
hardware
   computing devices 61–4
   input devices 52–5
   output devices 57–60
health and safety, of ICT systems 111
Health and Safety at Work Act 1974 29–30
Health and Safety (Display Screen Equipment)
   Regulations 1992 30
Heathrow Airport Terminal 5 113, 115
hierarchical business structures 7–8
home pages 143
home working 115–16
hotspots 53
house style 123–4
human resources departments 7
hyperlinks 143–4

ICT systems
   case study examples of 88–9

Index

changing/improving
    consequences of 115–16
    implementing 113
    planning 112–13
costs of 110, 115
ease-of-use 110
environmental sustainability 111
failure/success, reasons for 110–11
fitness for purpose 110–11
health and safety 111
life cycle of 112
security 38, 51, 62, 74–9, 111
testing 113
indexing, in manual storage systems 48
information, access to 34–6
Information Commissioner 34, 36
information management
    computer-based systems 50–1
    manual systems 47–8, 51
information storage
    computer-based storage devices 66–7
    computer-based systems 50–1
    manual systems 47–8, 51
inkjet printers 59
input devices 52–5
internet *see also* websites
    internet service providers (ISP) 80
    payment systems 80, 82
intranets 94, 115, 168
investment 10

joysticks 54

key field 156
keyboards 52–3

laptop computers 63–4
laser printers 59
law, impact on businesses of
    consumer protection 32–3, 45
    copyright, and data storage 37–8
    data protection/access to information 34–6
    employment law 26–7
    environmental protection 40–1
    health and safety at work 28–30
layering, in DTP 133, 136
layout
    presentations 138

webpages 144
leaflets 97
letters, business 97, 120–2
liquid crystal display (LCD) monitors 57
logos 130–1

magnetic tape 66
mail-merge 159–61
mailshots 92, 97
malware 74–5, 78
managers 7–8, 105
    network managers 51, 76–7
manual storage/filing systems 47–8
    computer-based systems compared 51
market
    defining 21
    influences on 12–13
market research 22
market share 10, 21–2
marketing 7, 24–5
    blogs/wikis as 167–8
Marks and Spencer Plc 36
Master Slides 138, 140, 144
maternity/paternity leave 26–7
meetings 95–6, 99
    and diary management software 163–4
    minutes 126
    notices of/agenda 125–6
memorandum/memo 93, 123–4
memory cards/sticks 67, 72
mice 53
microfilm 47–8
microphones 45
Microsoft 21–2
Microsoft Outlook ® 163–4
minutes, of meetings 126
mobile phones 100–1
modems 80
monitors 30, 56–7
monopolies 21
motherboards 61
multi-part stationery 60
multi-tasking 115
mystery shoppers 17, 21

narration, in presentations 139
netbooks 63
networks 50

Index

benefits/drawbacks 62
fileservers 62, 77
managers 51, 76–7
routers 62
newsletters 93, 135–6
not-for-profit organisations 4
notice boards 94
notice of meeting 125

objectives, of business 10–11
OCR (optical character recognition) 55
operating system software 61
operatives 7–8
optical character recognition (OCR) 55
optical disks 69–70, 72
output devices 57–60

packaging 24, 41
panel interviews 15
parental/paternity leave 26–7
partnerships 4–5
passwords 76
pay 26
payment systems
    electronic point of sale (EPOS) devices 64
    internet/e-commerce 80, 82
PayPal 80
personal digital assistants (PDA) 63–4, 101
phishing 74
pixels 45
plasma screen monitors 57
point of sale promotion 24
portable flash drives 67
presentation software 138–41
    animation/narration in 139, 140–1
    benefits/drawbacks 139
    common mistakes made using 139
    features of 138–9
presentations 95
prices
    and competitiveness 24
    price comparison surveys/websites 21
primary key 156
printers 59–60
private limited companies 5
production departments 7
products
    development, and competitiveness 25

product life 25
quality/safety of 32–3
testing, and customer satisfaction 17
profits 4, 10
project management software 165–6
projects, defining 165
public limited companies (PLC) 5
public sector organisations 4
punctuation 44, 120
purchasing departments 7

questionnaires 15–16, 22–3
QWERTY keyboards 52–3

radio-frequency identification (RFID) systems 104
re-skilling 115
recruitment 28
recycling 40–1
redundancy 27, 116
relative cell referencing 148–9
remote data storage 66, 72–3
remote working 115–16
removable storage media 66–7
repeat business 20
reports, business 93–4
resizing graphics 129
RFID (radio-frequency identification systems) 104
risk assessments 29–30
routers, network 62

sales departments 7
satellite navigation systems 103–4
scanners 54–5
school office, ICT systems in 88
secret shoppers 17, 21
security, of ICT systems 38, 51, 62, 74–9, 111
servers 50, 62, 77, 80
shareholders 5
silent-calling 100
social responsibility 42–3
software 61, 78
    software audits 38
sole traders 4, 7
sorting
    databases 155–6
    spreadsheets 150–1
sound cards 62
SPAM 74–5, 78

Index

span of control 8
speakers 60
spelling errors 44
spreadsheets 146–52
   benefits/drawbacks 152
   cell referencing 148–9
   formulae in 147–50
   inserting/deleting data 149–50
   sorting 150–1
spyware 74, 78
stakeholders 105–6
stand-by mode 111
storage media
   computer-based 66–7, 69–70
   manual 47
   remote storage 70
supervisors 7–8
suppliers 11, 105, 108
sustainable development 40–1
system administrators 76
systems life cycle 112

tabs 133–4
telephones, communication by 96
   effective, rules for 99–100
   mobile phones 100–1
   telephone/video conferencing 96, 103
templates 120, 132, 134, 138
text-to-speech software 60
thermal printers 59
'to do' lists 164
tone, errors of 44
toner 59
toolbars 132–3
touch-screen devices 53
trade unions 28
training 18, 115, 127

ultra density optical discs (UDO) 70
uncertainty, in business 12–13
unique record identifiers 156
unlimited liability 4–5
usernames 76

value for money 21, 105
verbal communication
   external 99–100
   internal 95–6
   telephone/video calls 96, 99–100, 103
video cards 62
video conferencing 96, 103
Virgin 13
viruses 38, 74, 78
visual aids 95
visual display units 30, 56–7
voice recognition software 45

Waste Electrical and Electronic Equipment (WEEE) Directive 2003 40–1
web creation software 143–5
web servers 80
webcams 45
websites 80–1, 98, 143
   benefits/drawbacks 145
   customer service feedback 17
   price comparison websites 21, 81
   security of 79
   web creation software 143–5
wikis 168
wireless technology
   input devices 52–3
   wireless networks 62
wizards 133
word-of-mouth recommendation 20
workstations 62
written communication
   e-mail 74–5, 94, 98, 123, 163–4
   external 97–8, 167–8
   flyers/leaflets/brochures 97, 134–6
   house style 123–4
   internal 93–4
   letters 97, 120–2
   mailshots 92, 97
   memorandum/memo 93, 123–4
   newsletters 93, 135–6
   reports 93–4

Yahoo 72

zooming, text 136